MW01061754

Glaciers!

The Art of Travel & the Science of Rescue

Michael Strong

Eck Doerry

Illustrations by Ryan Ojerio

FALCON®

Guilford, Connecticut

An imprint of The Globe Pequot Press

AFALCONGUIDE®

Library of Congress Cataloging-in-Publication Data is available.

ISBN 1-58592-054-1

Manufactured in the United States of America
First Edition/First Printing

CAUTION
Outdoor recreational activities are by their very nature potentially hazardous. All participants in such activities must assume the responsibility for their own actions and safety. The information contained in this guidebook cannot replace sound judgment and good decision-making skills, which help reduce risk exposure, nor does the scope of this book allow for disclosure of all the potential hazards and risks involved in such activities.

Learn as much as possible about the outdoor recreational activities in which you participate, prepare for the unexpected, and be cautious. The reward will be a safer and more enjoyable experience.

CONTENTS

INTRODUCTION 1

1 GLACIER FEATURES AND HAZARDS.........................3
Genesis and Flow of Alpine Glaciers............................3
Glacier Hazards..5
    Crevasses..5
    Other Hazards...10

2 EQUIPMENT AND CLOTHING..............................13
Rope Selection...13
The Harness System 14
The Ice Axe 17
Crampons...19
Ascenders 22
    Friction Knots 22
        Cordage 22
    Mechanical Ascenders.......................................23
        Mini Ascenders..................................25
Pulleys..26
Clothing 26

3 RIGGING FOR GLACIER TRAVEL AND RESCUE 29
Configuring the Rope for Travel.................................30
    Spacing and Placement of Climbers
        along the Rope..30
    Availability of Rope for Rescue............................31
    The Number of Climbers on a Rope 31
        The Two-Person Rope Team......................31
        The Three-Person Rope Team....................32
        The Four- or Five-Person Rope Team........32
Attaching to the Rope...32
Rigging with Prusik knots and Mechanical
    Ascenders...34
    Rigging with Prusik Knots 34
        The Seat Harness Prusik...........................34
        The Foot Prusik..34

Height and Reach of the Prusiks...............36
Arrangement of the Prusiks on the
    Rope...36
The Middle Person......................................37
Rigging with Mechanical Ascenders...................38
Rigging with an Ascender and a Prusik Cord....38
Rigging a Ropeman or Tibloc Ascender.............38
Rigging with a Heavy Pack.................................39
The Pack Prusik and Tether 40
Pack Tether Clipped to the Clip-in Knot.............40
Pack Tethered with the Rope End......................41
Pack Tether Clipped to the Climbing Rope........41
Which Rigging Option to Choose? 42
Rigging Considerations for Sled Use 42
Rigging a Sled 43
Sled Prusik...43
Rigging with a Butterfly Knot....................43
Attaching with Clove Hitches.....................44
The Buddy System 45
Rescue Gear 45

4 ANCHORS...47
Anchor Points..47
Anchors for Soft Snow 47
Snow Flukes...47
Deadman Anchors......................................50
Anchors for Firm Snow..51
Pickets 51
Firn Tubes..52
Ice Anchors 52
Ice Screws 52
Bollards—Anchors for Ice or Snow 53
Anchor Systems 54
Self-Equalizing Anchor System............................54
Position Equalized Anchor 56
Tensioned Back-up..56

5 GLACIER TRAVEL TECHNIQUES 59
Routefinding 59
Rope Management 61
Circumventing Crevasses 62
    End Runs 62
    Traveling in Echelon 63
        Practicing Rope Management 64
Crossing Crevasses 64
    Snowbridges 64
    Jumping Across 65
Belaying 67
    Belay Systems for Low-force Falls 70
        The Self-Arrest 70
        The Prusik Self-Belay 70
        Belaying a Teammate with the
           Harness Prusik 71
    Anchored Belays—Systems for
      Moderate- and High-Force Falls 73
        The Boot-Axe Belay 74
        The Harness-Axe Belay 75
        The Running Belay 76
        Belaying from an Anchor System 77
Travel During Inclement Weather 79
        Making Wands 80
Traveling on Skis or Snowshoes 80
Camping on the Glacier 82

6 CREVASSE RESCUE 85
A. Self-Rescue—An Overview 86
    The Self-Rescue Sequence for a Fallen
      Climber 86
        Practicing Fixed-Rope Ascension 89
    Self-Rescue with a Heavy Pack 90
    Ascending Past a Sled 90
B. Crevasse Rescue—An Overview 93
    Tension-Release Knots—Essential
      Components of Rescue Systems 95

Rescue Systems for a Rope Team of Three
or More 98

Basic Systems: C-Pulley and Z-Pulley
Rescues 100

The C-Pulley Rescue 100

Converting the C-Pulley to a
Z-Pulley 102

The Z-Pulley Rescue....................................103

Hauling without Pulleys............................105

Using a Directional.....................................107

Managing an Entrenched Rope 108

Recovering after Hoisting a Climber
into an Overhang 108

Combining Pulley Systems: Solutions for
Heavy Hauling...110

Adding on to a C-Pulley 111

Adding on to a Z-Pulley.............................114

Special Problems 116

The Bilgeri Rescue......................................116

Lack of Working Space 118

Uphill Rescues 119

Rescuing the Middle Person.....................123

Rescuing the Middle Person: Some
Important Considerations.....................128

Rappelling to Aid an Unconscious
Climber 129

Rescuing a Climber Pulling a Sled 135

Rescue Systems for a Two-Person Rope Team.........136

The Lone Rescuer or Canadian Drop
Loop System 136

Increasing the Efficiency of the Lone
Rescuer Drop Loop System.................140

Other Considerations for Two-Person
Rescue 140

APPENDIX 1: KNOTS FOR GLACIER TRAVEL
AND RESCUE..142
Knot Selection and Care 142
    Bends, Loops, and Hitches........................142
    Performance Qualities 143
    Knot Management......................................144
Suggested Knots for Travel and Rescue..................146
    Tie-in and Clip-in Knots 146
    Friction Knots 147
    Useful Hitches...148
    Other Useful Knots 152
    Webbing Knots...153

APPENDIX 2: THE SELF-ARREST...........................155
Self-Arrest Techniques.......................................156
    The Basic Self-Arrest Position 156
    Feet-First Fall...156
    Head-First Downhill on the Stomach............157
    Head-First Downhill on the Back 157
    Self-Arrest with a Large Pack......................158
    Common Self-Arrest Mistakes.....................159
    Suggestions for Making Self-Arrest
      Practice More Challenging 160
    Self-Arrests and Crampons.........................160

APPENDIX 3: MECHANICAL ADVANTAGE 161
Common Rescue Systems 161
    The 1:1 System..161
    C-Pulley..162
    C-Pulley on a C-Pulley...............................162
    Z-Pulley 163
    Z-Pulley with a Ratchet Prusik.....................164
    The 6:1 System...164

BIBLIOGRAPHY..166
ABOUT THE AUTHORS AND ILLUSTRATOR 167

Introduction

Glaciers are common features of alpine environments. Whether mountaineering in the Alaska range or out for a weekend climb in the Cascades, chances are that sooner or later you'll have to cross a glacier. Consequently, a solid understanding of glacier travel procedures and crevasse rescue techniques should be part of every mountaineer's repertoire.

Attitudes toward glacier travel vary widely. For some climbers, glaciers are impediments to be crossed as quickly as possible while en route to a distant summit; for others, glacier travel provides adventure and reward in its own right. Some climbers are apprehensive about the dangers posed by glacier travel, whereas others don't give them a second thought.

These diverse attitudes are often reflected in the way people travel on glaciers. It's not uncommon to see climbers traveling alone, relying on nothing more than their routefinding abilities and good luck to provide safe passage over and around the various obstacles and hazards. At the other extreme are rope teams whose members understand the intricacies of glacier flow, know how to travel safely over glaciated terrain, and are capable of efficiently rescuing a team member from a crevasse. Most glacier travelers fall somewhere in the middle: The majority of these hikers and climbers carry ice axes, ropes, and other gear, but lack the skills needed to arrest a fall or rescue a climber who has fallen into a crevasse.

In certain respects glacier travel is like a game of chess. The rope team's knowledge, skill, and strategy are pitted against the glacier's routefinding challenges and hazards. A team that makes correct decisions is more likely to be rewarded with safe passage; a team that ignores or misreads the subtle clues found in the glacial terrain will quite likely suffer the consequences of a crevasse fall.

Of course, there are no guarantees; even skilled mountaineers occasionally find themselves dangling in the abyss. One thing is certain; if you spend enough time traveling on glaciers, at some point you'll either personally inspect the interior of a crevasse or work to rescue a fallen partner from one.

Hopefully you'll be prepared for this moment. A conceptual understanding of crevasse rescue is a critical first step in this situation—you need to know what to do. But you must also be skilled enough to deal with adverse circumstances calmly and efficiently, and experienced enough to implement the correct rescue response. Knowledge goes only so far. It's but one side of the safety triangle; skill and experience complete the trinity.

The upper Susitna Glacier—Mount Hayes in the distance. Tony Jewell photo

So, what's the underskilled and inexperienced novice to do? Start by reading this book with the understanding that knowledge is critical, but is by no means a substitute for field experience. Then put in hours on the practice slope honing your skills. Make your practice sessions situation specific. For example, if you plan on traveling as an independent rope team of two, then practice rigging and rescue techniques specific to a two-person rope team. When you're face down in the snow in self-arrest, facing the daunting task of having to place an anchor while continuing to hold your fallen partner, you'll be very glad for every second spent practicing for this very situation.

Once you have studied and practiced the basic techniques, you'll be ready to explore a real glacier. But don't be too hasty! Start conservatively and travel with others who are more experienced. The world of snow and ice offers almost limitless possibilities for adventure and enjoyment, at a minimal risk to those willing to invest in the skills and knowledge necessary for safe glacier travel.

Glacier Features and Hazards

CHAPTER 1

GENESIS AND FLOW OF ALPINE GLACIERS

Alpine glaciers are formed in mountainous regions when snow accumulation exceeds snow loss over long periods of time. Accumulation may be the result of snowfall, avalanches, or wind deposition. The snow is eventually compressed into ice, and when the pressure reaches a critical point in the lower reaches of the icepack it becomes viscous (like toothpaste) and may start to flow. Alpine glaciers are essentially rivers of ice, flowing imperceptibly down the valleys in which they lie. Although they often appear similar, glaciers should not be confused with *permanent snowfields*. Snowfields don't have enough ice to move, or they sit in confining basins, making flow impossible.

Figure 1-1. Common features of an alpine glacier.

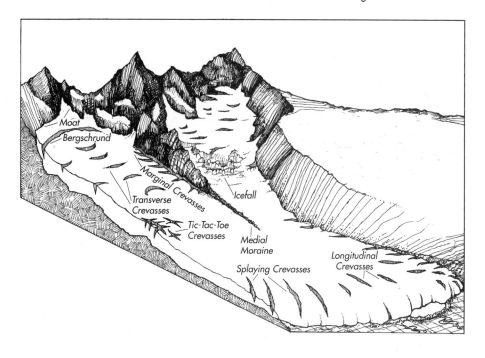

The size of an alpine glacier and the distance it moves depend largely on the climate. If snow consistently accumulates at the glacier's head, the ice formed feeds the glacier and pushes it along. During a warming climatic trend, the pace of melting outstrips the accumulation of snow and ice, and the glacier recedes.

On a smaller scale, the appearance of a glacier changes with the seasons. Melting, or *ablation* is an annual process on all but the coldest of glaciers. Under the influence of summer's warmth the edge of the previous winter's snow cover recedes up the glacier, exposing old snow layers or even bare ice. By fall this snow line may be well up the glacier; after a particularly warm summer, all of the previous year's snow may have melted.

The dynamics of glacier movement can best be described as the interaction of three distinct factors:

Channeled flow:

Flowing in a channel carved by its own movement, the behavior of an alpine glacier closely resembles that of a river. The bottom and side boundaries of the channel restrict flow and exert differential pressures on the mass of moving ice, resulting in varying rates of flow within the glacier. As in a river, the area of fastest movement is near the surface and in the middle of the glacier, while flow is slower near the edges. As the glacier curves, flow is fastest on the outside radius of the curve and slowest on the inside.

Slope variations:

When a river slows down a "backwater effect" is produced and the river becomes deeper. Similarly, when a glacier slows down over a gentle section, the ice is squeezed together and the glacier becomes thicker. This is known as *compressive flow.* Conversely, when a glacier passes over a steeper area it speeds up, stretches out, and becomes thinner. This is called *extending flow.*

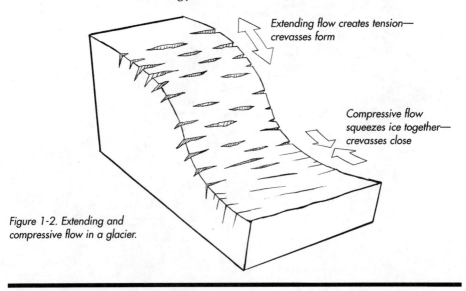

Extending flow creates tension—
crevasses form

Compressive flow
squeezes ice together—
crevasses close

Figure 1-2. Extending and
compressive flow in a glacier.

Midstream obstacles:

When a river encounters an underwater obstacle, water is forced over and around it, producing a wave; the larger the obstacle, the larger the wave. When a glacier confronts a resistant obstacle (e.g., a bulge of harder rock that it cannot pluck away), it is forced upward into a moundlike (convex) shape.

Crevasses form in areas where the effects of one (or more) of the above factors create tension zones within the glacier, causing the ice to crack open. Let's take a closer look at how and where crevasses form and review a number of other hazards encountered during glacier travel.

GLACIER HAZARDS

Compared with the steep, rugged terrain of surrounding ridgelines and faces, glaciers can provide convenient access to the mountainous interior, stretching like superhighways through difficult country. In many areas, a glacier is the only realistic option (short of an airlift) for approaching a climb. Unfortunately, the innocuous appearance of a glacier can be extremely deceptive; countless alpine travelers have lost their lives to crevasse falls, avalanches, icefalls, and other hazards. In fact, the hazards of glacier travel can be just as lethal as those encountered on steeper terrain and perhaps even more dangerous because they are much less apparent.

CREVASSES

Crevasses are the most frequently encountered travel hazard. While a fall into a crevasse is a potential hazard almost anywhere on a glacier, the danger is greatly increased in the

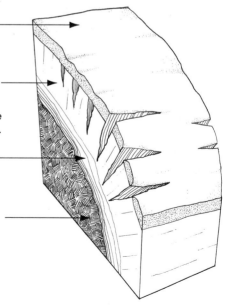

Surface snow—can hide crevasses, making travel dangerous.

Upper ice layer—brittle and prone to splitting open (into crevasses) when the glacier "bends" at zones of tension. Approximately 100 feet thick.

Lower ice layer—a dense plastic layer. Pressure from overlying ice prevents crevasses from forming. Rock and other debris carried in this layer scrape away layers of adjacent rock.

Bedrock—the glacier carves a region's bedrock into a variety of geographic formations such as aretes (ridges), horns (sharp summits), and vertical cliffs. It also carries debris that eventually gets "stockpiled" into moraines.

Figure 1-3. Cross-section of an alpine glacier.

accumulation zone, where crevasses may be hidden beneath a weak layer of surface snow. When crevasses are clearly visible and the surface is not steep, it's usually safe to walk about without the security of a rope. A thorough understanding of where crevasses are likely to occur and how to detect their presence beneath the snow is your first and best defense for safe passage.

In general, crevasses form *perpendicular* to tension, though in some cases the complex forces resulting from a merging of two or more tension zones result in seemingly chaotic arrays of crevasses. The depth of a crevasse depends on the underlying terrain and the speed of glacier movement. Crevasses are seldom deeper than about 100 feet, as ice below this depth is under enough pressure to keep it from fracturing. The most common tension zones are:

- within areas of extending flow (where the slope steepens);
- on the sides of the glacier where friction with the rock wall is encountered;
- where the valley containing a glacier narrows or widens;
- where the glacier flows around a bend; or
- over and around midstream obstacles.

Certain types of crevasses are associated with each of these tension zones. It's important to note, however, that on an actual glacier each zone is unique; complex interactions of terrain, ice, and gravity sometimes result in unexpected fracture patterns.

Transverse crevasses form as a result of extending flow, which produces longitudinal tension in the glacier. To visualize this, bend a soft candy bar gently. Cracks form in the outer surface when the bar is bent, with the widest openings corresponding to the zone of greatest tension or bend. Transverse crevasses are usually concave in shape when first formed, with the arcs oriented down-glacier like frowns. Over time, the arcs may slowly be transformed into straight lines (or even convex arcs) by the faster movement of the ice near the center of the flow.

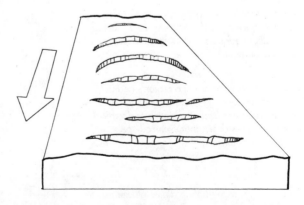

Figure 1-4. Orientation of transverse crevasses during flow.

Marginal crevasses form at the tension zone created between the faster-moving central ice and ice slowed by friction with the glacier's confining sidewall. This discrepancy in flow rates produces herringbone crevasses, which angle approximately 45 degrees up-glacier. Over time, the crevasses are usually rotated down-glacier by the faster-moving central ice stream. When they have been rotated approximately 30 degrees (so they are still oriented slightly up-glacier), a new set of crevasses opens. As a result, sets of intersecting crevasses are common on the glacier's flanks, making travel very difficult in this region.

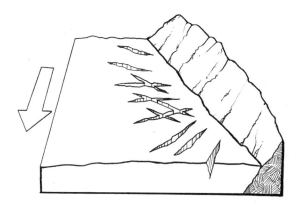

Figure 1-5. Marginal crevasses.

When a glacier is free to spread out (e.g., at the terminus, or anywhere lateral confinement is reduced), tension is across the glacier (rather than along it), and *longitudinal* crevasses may form, running parallel to the flow of the glacier. Moderate compressive flow also extends the glacier sideways (unless the glacier is completely constrained by the channel), producing *splaying* crevasses, which start out longitudinally and curve around into a diagonal orientation at the margins.

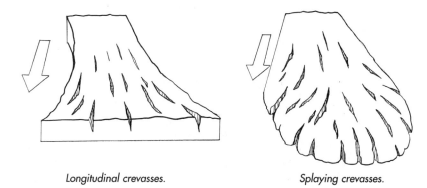

Longitudinal crevasses.   Splaying crevasses.

Figure 1-6. Longitudinal and splaying crevasses.

Other types of crevasses to look out for are *radial* crevasses, which form on the outside of bends and look like spokes on a wheel, and *tic-tac-toe* crevasses, which form as the glacier bulges over an underlying rock knob and resemble, as the name implies, the cross-hatched pattern of a tic-tac-toe game.

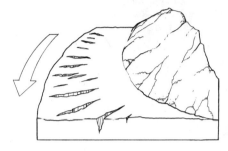

Radial crevasses.

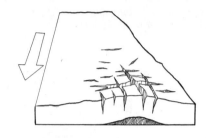

Tic-tac-toe crevasses.

Figure 1-7. Radial and tic-tac-toe crevasses.

Whereas moderate compressive flow closes crevasses, the opposite effect results when compressive flow is extreme. For example, where the speed of the glacier slows dramatically, or when two glaciers meet and compress together, a jumble of crevasses is created. Moving through this mess of crevasses is extremely difficult, if not impossible.

When extending flow is extreme, such as in very steep areas, an *icefall* is produced. The only way through an icefall that cannot be circumvented is to climb down, up, and over the jumble of ice blocks. Particularly dangerous hazards within icefalls are *seracs,* large free-standing towers of leaning ice that may topple at any moment as the glacier creeps along.

The *bergschrund* is the highest crevasse on the glacier, formed where the glacier separates itself from the stationary snow or ice above. The bergschrund should not be confused with the *moat,* which is the space between the edge of the glacier and the adjacent rock wall. Unlike the bergschrund, which is the result of tension, the moat is formed by the reflective warmth of the sun on nearby rock. Both the moat and the bergschrund can create significant obstacles to leaving or gaining access to the glacier, especially later in the day when warming is most likely to have weakened snowbridges.

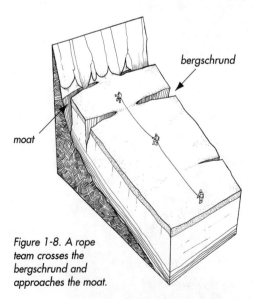

bergschrund

moat

Figure 1-8. A rope team crosses the bergschrund and approaches the moat.

Wading through a slush pool, lower reach of the Muldrow Glacier, Denali. Michael Strong photo

OTHER HAZARDS

Although crevasses are usually the most significant travel hazard, a number of other common features can be dangerous as well. These features must be carefully considered when planning a route on the glacier.

Surface ice in the ablation zone usually offers surprisingly good footing, especially after it has been weathered by the sun and, in some cases, dusted with a summer's worth of airborne grit and dust. After a rain, however, the weathered ice can be quickly washed away, leaving a slick, mirrored surface. At these times, crampons may be needed to move safely on even the most level surface.

On larger glaciers, *meltwater streams* can sometimes be large enough to impede travel. The risks of wading or jumping over a meltwater stream are considerable, so use caution when confronted with a stream that is too large to hop comfortably across. The creek bed will likely be extremely slippery and it's usually not worth the risk of falling in and being swept downstream. At worst, you could be carried into a *moulin,* a pothole carved in the ice by the swirling water. Some moulins spiral down into the glacier's depths, like gigantic bathtub drains. Often the safest course of action is to follow the stream down-glacier, where it will eventually be swallowed up by a moulin or crevasse.

On flatter terrain, slush and meltwater may collect in large puddles and small pools. These are most commonly found just below the snowline where melting is most active, and can be difficult to detect, especially following a heavy snowfall. Watch for darker areas on the surface of the snow; if water seeps into the freshly made footsteps of the leader, it may be time to call a hasty retreat. In many cases, the affected area is so extensive that there is no choice but to travel through the icy water and slush. Remove boot liners to keep them dry, use a ski pole (or something similar) for balance and support, and prepare for a numbing experience. Although the discomfort will be intense, it is important to resist the urge to plunge ahead. Move slowly and probe the surface carefully to detect hidden holes.

When circumventing a crevasse isn't possible or practical, the best option may be to find a suitable *snowbridge.* The strength of snowbridges varies widely, depending on such factors as their thickness, the time of year, and even the time of day. Techniques for assessing and crossing snowbridges are discussed in chapter 5.

The steep ridges and faces that confine a glacier are subject to avalanches, icefall, and rockfall. Snow, ice, or rock falling from surrounding heights can reach surprisingly far across the relatively flat surface of a glacier. These hazards should be carefully considered when planning a route, making routefinding decisions, and establishing campsites. Look for old debris and other clues to detect danger zones and avoid routes that run beneath walls or steep slopes, particularly on the side of the valley most exposed to the sun, or any slope that might pose a significant avalanche hazard. If travel through such danger zones is unavoidable, consider traveling at night (if it's light enough), when snow and ice are more stable. In any case, it's best not to linger in these areas; move quickly through them to a safer area. A course in avalanche safety (and regular review) should be considered basic prerequisites for glacier travel.

As a glacier moves along, the tremendous pressure exerted by the moving ice carves away at the channel containing the glacier. The resulting debris is carried along until it is either pushed out to the side of the flow or deposited at the snout, where the glacier ends. These mounds of glacier debris are known as *moraines* and are classified as lateral, medial, or terminal, depending on whether they appear on the sides, middle, or terminus of the glacier, respectively. Successive terminal moraines, called recessional moraines, commonly appear in the valley below the snout of a glacier, marking the retreat of the glacier over the course of several centuries.

A well-equipped glacier traveler. Michael Stong photo

Equipment and Clothing

The image that today's alpinist may recall from the early days of glacier travel is of a team of mountaineers trudging over the glacier with coils of rope around their waists and minimal (if any) rigging. While it may be nostalgic to picture the early climbers roped together in this fashion, it must also be remembered that many were seriously injured in crevasse falls; many climbers lost their lives due to inadequate clothing, "minimalist" rigging techniques, and scant knowledge of crevasse rescue procedures.

Although a "minimalist" approach to glacier travel is still attractive to some climbers, it's an invitation to injury, or worse. By adding just a few lightweight pieces of equipment and taking the time to learn the proper rigging and rescue techniques, the safety (not to mention comfort) of glacier travel can be dramatically improved. This chapter briefly reviews the equipment used by the modern glacier traveler and provides a comparative overview of different options.

ROPE SELECTION

When thinking of climbing equipment, a rope is usually the first item that comes to mind. In an activity in which gravity (i.e., falling) is the principal adversary, the rope is an essential item for protecting a team's safety. Selecting a rope for mountaineering can be difficult; at least 15 different rope companies advertise their products in the United States, each claiming advantages in strength, durability, and water resistance of their ropes over other brands.

It is difficult to choose one rope for all purposes. For glacier travel, the two most important characteristics of a rope are its length and diameter. Most North American climbers use large-diameter (10 to 11 mm) ropes for technical climbing as well as for glacier crossings en route to technical peak ascents.

If glacier travel is a priority, however, consider buying double 8.5 or 9 mm ropes. Although two 9 mm ropes are generally heavier than a single 11 mm rope, this small difference in weight is more than offset by the greater number of options available for rigging, climbing, and rescue. For glacier travel, where potential fall forces are relatively low, a single rope can be used, leaving the second rope available for rescue. For technical ice and rock climbs, the ropes can be doubled, opening more possibilities for arranging protection and adding a measure of redundancy in case one rope is damaged by rock fall or a stray crampon point. The ropes can be tied together for long rappels, avoiding the need to carry a second rope in addition to the main climbing rope. Use a 60 m rope because four or even five people can be spaced safely along its length. Even in smaller rope teams, a longer rope means that more rope is available for rescue.

A "dry" rope, which has been chemically treated for water resistance is well worth its slightly higher price. Since a rope's strength drops significantly when it becomes saturated with water (by as much as 30 percent), treated ropes are consistently stronger than untreated ones of the same diameter in a wet environment. A dry rope also remains lighter and easier to manage in below-freezing temperatures.

THE HARNESS SYSTEM

A well-designed harness is convenient to put on, comfortable to wear, and supportive during even the most forceful of falls. For many years, a harness was considered an unnecessary luxury. Climbers simply looped several coils around their waists and secured them with nonconstricting knots like a bowline on a coil, or a bowline on a bight (if roping into the middle). Though every climber should still know these knots for emergencies (and for their many other uses), they are now used as a means to tie into the rope by only the most stubborn traditionalists.

There are a number of compelling reasons to avoid tying the rope directly around the midsection. On a practical level, wrapping four to six coils of rope around the waist uses up 15 feet or more of valuable climbing rope, shortens the distance between belays on a technical climb (thereby slowing progress), and leaves less rope for rescue. The most serious drawback of tying directly into the rope, however, is that it is patently dangerous: During a fall, the coils tend to ride up around the fallen climber's chest, constricting breathing and leading to slow asphyxiation. In head-first falls, there is a very real danger of slipping right out of the coils. Finally, as discussed in upcoming sections, it's sometimes more sensible to clip into the rope (i.e., using a locking carabiner) than to tie in; obviously, this requires wearing a harness of some kind.

Most climbers opt for a lightweight harness of some sort. For just a few ounces of extra weight, the comfort and reliability of the climber's attachment to the rope are greatly improved. There are three basic harness systems to choose from: a seat harness alone, a combination seat and chest harness, or a full-body harness.

Most North American climbers use a *seat harness* for rock climbing and mountaineering. A seat harness is generally adequate for glacier travel as well, provided your harness is very supportive, you're not top-heavy (e.g., carrying a substantial pack), and the risk of falling into a crevasse is relatively small.

The seat harness must fit correctly, with the waist belt secured above the hip bones, providing a high tie-in point. A harness with a wide hip belt and broad leg loops provides a greater surface area to support your weight than one constructed from narrow strands of webbing, enhancing comfort during a fall. Leg loops that unbuckle make it much easier to don the harness while wearing crampons, to adjust clothing layers, and to answer the call of nature while staying tied in. Other useful features include gear loops for attaching rescue gear and a buckle system located away from the hip bones, so it will not interfere with the waist belt of a pack.

The risk of injury dramatically increases when you wear just a seat harness while carrying a heavy pack. A crevasse fall could easily result in violent hyperextension of the back, or even strip off your seat harness. When carrying a heavy pack, always wear a chest harness of some kind.

A *combination seat and chest harness* prevents backward rotation and reduces the chance of injury. The seat and chest portions should **never** be tied together to form a body harness with a single high attachment point. With a high tie-in point, a self-arrester will be pulled into a head-first position when someone on the rope team falls into a crevasse. The resulting awkward position makes it extremely difficult to self-arrest and initiate a rescue. Another danger of a high tie-in point is the excessive rotational "snap" exerted on the fallen climber, which greatly increases the potential for spinal injury.

The proper way to rig a combination chest and seat harness is to tie (or clip) into the seat harness and then clip the rope(s) through a carabiner on the chest harness. In this system, the chest harness acts as a directional, righting the climber during a fall, while leaving most of the force to be absorbed by the seat harness closer to the center of gravity.

Unless you plan to spend a lot of time on a glacier, there is no need to buy a commercial chest harness; an effective alternative can easily be improvised using one-inch tubular webbing. Two commonly used systems are shown below.

Figure 2-1. Crossed sling chest harness.

The *crossed sling* method is easy to put on and take off and is the simplest to tie. Cross the sling into a figure of eight configuration, lift it overhead and slide the arms through each of the loops. A significant disadvantage of this method is that the sling rides up when you're suspended, forcing the arms over the head, compromising arm movement and restricting breathing. More than one climber has had a tooth knocked out by the carabiner on the sling as it snaps upward when suddenly loaded during a crevasse fall.

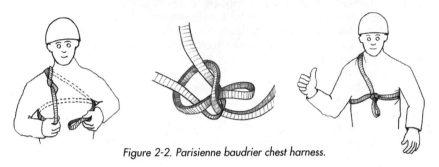

Figure 2-2. Parisienne baudrier chest harness.

The *Parisienne baudrier* does not ride up when loaded, as it is tied securely beneath the arms (Fig. 2-2). A common problem encountered when tying the baudrier, however, is ending up with a clip-in loop that hangs too low, essentially rendering the chest harness ineffective. This problem is easily remedied by tying off the excess webbing (around the control knot) with half hitches. Don't clip the guide carabiner through a chest strand of the baudrier instead of the loop (as a means of shortening the clip-in); this allows the carabiner to slide laterally under tension.

Tie the baudrier with an appropriate length of 1-inch tubular webbing. The amount of webbing needed depends upon the thickness of upper body layers worn. Since the chest harness is likely to be used in a variety of weather conditions, tie it over the layers worn in inclement weather. During more favorable conditions reduce the sling diameter for a proper fit.

Commercially made chest harnesses are popular with climbers who spend a great deal of time on big glaciers. They're fast to put on and take off and easy to adjust for correct fit when upper body layers need to be removed or added throughout the day. With any chest harness, make sure that it's snug (yet not so tight that it restricts breathing) and does not ride up when loaded.

The *full-body harness* is currently the only UIAA- (Union of International Alpine Associations) approved harness system. Though undoubtedly very secure, we find it difficult to recommend a full body harness for glacier travel. In addition to the previously noted disadvantages of a high tie-in point, full body harnesses do not allow for the easy addition or removal of extra layers, are more expensive, and are generally quite heavy. For these reasons, they are used most frequently in rescue and instructional scenarios, where absolute security is the prime consideration.

THE ICE AXE

The ice axe (Fig. 2-4) is the universal tool of the mountaineer, used for everything from self-belays and arrests to chopping steps and platforms. For glacier travel, the main consideration in selecting an ice axe is length. When the axe is held in the self-arrest position the spike should extend out just past your hip. Anything shorter increases the risk of self-impalement while self-arresting during a bad fall; anything much longer is cumbersome to manage.

Other features to look for include a smooth shaft that slides easily into hard snow when probing for crevasses or providing a boot-axe belay, a flat head that is comfortable on the palm when plunging the axe into the snow, a pick with negative clearance (so the axe isn't wrenched from your hands during self-arrest), and a head made from a steel or iron alloy that is riveted to the shaft. If saving weight is important, it's possible to get a durable, well-balanced mountaineering axe that weighs not much more than a pound!

Figure 2-3. Correct ice axe length when held in self-arrest position.

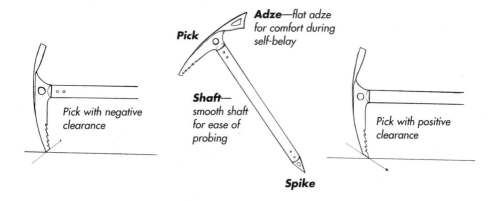

Pick

Adze—flat adze for comfort during self-belay

Pick with negative clearance

Shaft—smooth shaft for ease of probing

Pick with positive clearance

Spike

Figure 2-4. The ideal ice axe for glacier travel.

Avoid technical ice tools, especially the bent-shafted designs. They are too short for safe and effective self-arrest and the curved shaft makes it difficult to probe for crevasses or plunge the shaft into the snow for self-belay or anchoring.

The way you hold an ice axe is a matter of personal preference and situational necessity. Some climbers advocate the *self-arrest grip* with the adze pointing forward during travel and the palm resting over the much thinner pick. When held this way, it's easy to swing the axe quickly into the cross-body position for self-arrest. The drawback is that this grip is very uncomfortable on the palm when plunging the axe in for a boot-axe belay, a self-belay, or when probing for crevasses. Once your palm begins to hurt, your axe placements may become insecure and probes ineffective. For this very reason, many climbers opt for the *self-belay grip*—pick forward with the palm resting more comfortably on top of the adze. When held in self -belay, however, the axe must be quickly spun into self-arrest position during an unexpected fall, a task that calls for a well-conditioned response (Fig. 2-5).

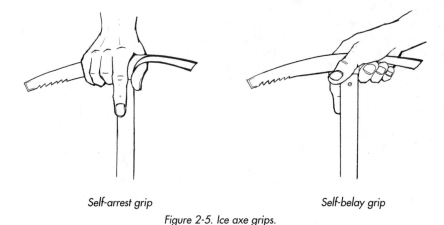

Self-arrest grip   Self-belay grip

Figure 2-5. Ice axe grips.

While on the glacier the main concern is being ready to arrest a team member who falls into a crevasse. It's best, therefore, to hold your axe with a self-arrest grip. When probing a snowbridge, executing a boot axe belay, or protecting your passage on a steep traverse, hold your axe appropriately—in self-belay.

In most alpine travel scenarios, common sense dictates that the ice axe not be attached to your body; having it flailing about during a tumbling fall poses a severe hazard. Such falls, however, are not likely while traveling on a glacier. The primary concern during glacier travel is to avoid losing the axe during a crevasse fall; an ice axe dropped on a mountainside can often be retrieved, one dropped into a crevasse will be lost forever. A lost axe creates a substantial liability for a rope team, because you'll be unable to help arrest any future crevasse falls. Because it is difficult to have the presence of mind to hold on to the axe during a crevasse fall, it's important to tether the ice axe in some way.

An axe tether with a wrist loop is a popular choice among North American climbers. Tie the wrist loop using 9/16- or 1-inch tubular webbing rather than round accessory cord, as webbing is more comfortable on the wrist. The loop must be snug enough to prevent the axe from being pulled from the wrist during a forceful crevasse fall. Do not use a cinch knot to snug the loop onto the wrist, as this makes removal of the axe more difficult, particularly in wet or icy conditions.

The tether should be long enough to permit switching the ice axe from hand to hand without removing the wrist loop.

Since an axe should be held in the uphill hand while traversing a slope, it may be necessary to switch hands often when weaving through a crevasse field or zigzagging a slope. The tether should be long enough to make it easy to switch hands without compromising body position and balance, yet not so long that the webbing hangs below the spike of the axe when held vertically (Fig. 2-6).

Figure 2-6. A tethered ice axe held with a self-belay grip.

Some climbers find a wrist tether annoying; others are unconvinced that a wrist tether will stay on after a particularly hard fall into a crevasse. Viable alternatives to a wrist leash include clipping the axe to the seat or chest harness, or tethering it over the shoulder.

CRAMPONS

A common misconception among inexperienced climbers is that crampons are called for any time they are traveling on hard snow or ice. This is not the case. Crampons are only a way of creating extra traction in situations where the unaided boot sole cannot find adequate grip. In all other situations, strapping on crampons will result only in slower progress, increased discomfort, and greater chance of injury to the rope, clothing, and rope team members. When hard or icy surface conditions make footing tenuous, however, crampons may be the only way to move safely and efficiently over the ice. It may be necessary to put crampons on and take them off more than once in the course of a day, so make sure they allow easy placement and removal, and stay securely attached.

Two basic styles of crampon bindings are available (Fig. 2-7). *Step-in bindings* offer quick attachment and are an excellent choice in colder conditions, since there are no straps to constrict circulation or buckles to confound numb fingertips. Step-ins are relatively expensive, however, and require a stiff boot with a welt wide enough to solidly engage the bails that hold the crampon to the boot.

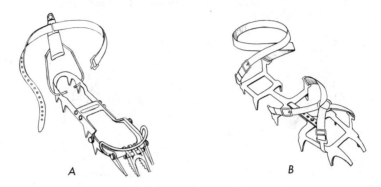

Figure 2-7. (A) Rigid crampons with step-in bindings and (B) hinged crampons with strap-on bindings (Scottish ring style)

Strap-on bindings are less expensive than step-ins but are less convenient to put on. There are several systems for rigging the straps attaching the crampons to the boot. Consider using the "Scottish ring" style, which has a center ring permanently positioned between the front posts of each crampon by short neoprene straps. This system reduces the time spent putting the crampons on, especially when wearing gloves. Make sure the buckles are oriented to the outside of the boot where they are less likely to be caught by a crampon point while climbing. After cinching the straps, tuck the ends out of the way, or cut them to an appropriate length ahead of time.

Crampons may be hinged or rigid. *Hinged* crampons are well suited for glacier travel and general mountaineering routes that do not involve a lot of front pointing because they flex and are more comfortable when walking. *Rigid* crampons can be worn only with very stiff, full shank boots (e.g., most plastic boots), which are usually not comfortable when worn over long distances.

Another feature to consider is the orientation of the two front points. Ordinarily, crampons designed for general mountaineering use have horizontal front points that provide good flotation in soft snow conditions. Crampons designed for climbing waterfall ice have vertical front points, necessary for penetration and purchase in harder ice conditions.

Take note of the following considerations related to crampon use:

- Do not step on the rope! This is one of the first habits that you should develop as a mountaineer, and is especially important when everyone is wearing crampons. Be observant while traveling and keep a sharp eye out for accidental damage caused by other team members. A rope that has been punctured by a crampon can no longer be trusted and should be retired immediately, or at least tied off at the point of puncture (with a butterfly knot as shown in Fig. 2-8), as it may be difficult to locate the damaged point once the sheath has worked back into position.

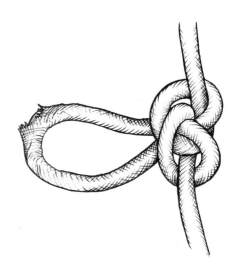

Figure 2-8. Isolating a damaged section of rope with a butterfly knot.

- Pay attention while walking. It's easy to catch a crampon point in clothing, especially with the uphill leg when traversing a slope. Wear long gaiters (or pants) that conform snugly to the legs in order to reduce the chance of catching a crampon point. High gaiters with a tough Cordura scuff guard on the inner leg have a much longer life span than flimsier models, and are far cheaper to replace than expensive outerwear.

- In warming conditions, snow may ball up under your foot. This can be extremely dangerous if it causes you to lose footing at a critical moment. Place a plastic bag, a thin sheet of plastic (e.g., a commercially designed antiballing snow plate or a piece of a bleach bottle), or even a piece of Ensolite pad between the boot sole and the crampon to reduce the possibility of excessive snow build-up. Another solution is to simply rap the crampon sharply with the shaft of the ice axe every so often. But be careful! Not only is it easy to lose your balance while cleaning crampons, it's possible to crack a plastic boot or bruise your shin with an overly aggressive or poorly aimed swing. It's also easy to dent, and thus weaken or ruin tubular aluminum ice axe shafts by striking the edge of a crampon.

- Self-arrest using the knees rather than the feet is crucial. It's extremely easy to catch a crampon point and break an ankle while self-arresting with your toes down. Using the knees for self-arrest is somewhat less effective, can be uncomfortable, and feels less natural than digging in the toes, but is crucial for avoiding serious injury. Practice is necessary to develop the correct reflex.

- Crampon repair in the field can be frustrating, so fit and tighten the crampons at home, and carry a crampon repair kit specific to the team's needs. Periodically check to be sure all of the screws and/or nuts are tight; they often work loose.

ASCENDERS

Ascenders are either knots or mechanical devices that grab the rope and allow a climber to move along it. A climber usually goes up, or "ascends" the rope, hence the name. In the context of glacier travel and rescue, ascenders are used for self- and partner belaying during travel, to ascend the rope after a crevasse fall, to transfer the weight of a fallen climber to an anchor, and to increase efficiency in rescue systems incorporating mechanical advantage. There are two kinds of ascenders: friction knots and mechanical ascenders.

Friction Knots

Friction knots are tied onto the rope and grip the rope when loaded. When the load is released and the knot is loosened, the rope slides freely through the knot (or the knot slides along the rope, depending on the application). There are several types of friction knots, some of which work better than others for rigging and rescue. Generally speaking, the prusik knot is the friction knot of choice when rigging for glacier travel. It is not, however, the only knot that can be used for rigging and rescue. The merits and limitations of various friction knots are described in appendix 1.

Cordage

Nylon accessory cord is by far the most common choice. It's inexpensive, relatively strong, and supple enough to grip the rope when loaded. Table 2-1 provides a comparison of the strengths of various diameters of accessory cord and webbing commonly used for rigging and rescue work.

Material	Cord Diameter	Breaking Strength
nylon accessory cord	5 mm	1150–1250 pounds
nylon accessory cord	6 mm	1500–1700 pounds
nylon accessory cord	7 mm	2100–2300 pounds
Spectra cord	5.5 mm	4500 pounds
nylon webbing	9/16 inch	approximately 2500 pounds
nylon webbing	1 inch	approximately 4000 pounds

Table 2-1. Relative strengths of accessory cord and webbing.

When selecting cordage for prusik slings, keep in mind that you'll use your prusiks not only for self-rescue, but in rescue systems utilizing mechanical advantage (where the load on a prusik can be multiplied several times a climber's body weight). Given this fact, and given that prusik slings weaken with age, sustained loads, repeated exposure to ultraviolet radiation, and use in general, it is recommended that you stay within the *safe working load* of the materials you have selected. Using safe working load as a guideline, the breaking strength of the material should be at least five times the maximum load placed upon it.

Use the largest diameter cord capable of securely gripping the rope. A good rule to follow is selecting a cord that is at least 3 mm smaller in diameter than the climbing rope. For example, 6 mm cord is suitable for use on 9 mm (or larger) rope; 7 mm cord is too thick to hold securely on 9 mm ropes, but works well on ropes 10 mm and up.

Another material that works well is 5.5 mm Spectra cord. It's much stronger than nylon accessory cord, more resistant to abrasion, and does not break down with repeated bending. The disadvantage of Spectra cord is that it is more expensive.

As Table 2-1 illustrates, the common diameters of cordage and sling webbing used by the glacier traveler are certainly strong enough for rigging and rescue work, with one possible exception: 5 mm cordage. Applying the concept of safe working load, the maximum recommended load on 5 mm cord is approximately 250 pounds, certainly enough for self rescue and for use when hoisting light loads (e.g., a climber with a light pack), but marginally acceptable for safe *repeated use* as a haul prusik in a system where heavy hauling is required (e.g., hoisting a heavy climber pulling a fully loaded sled). When heavy hauling is more than a remote possibility, climbers rigging on a small diameter rope (e.g., 8.5 mm) should use 5.5 mm Spectra cord. It is narrow enough to provide good grip and strong enough for heavy hauling (see appendix 2, Mechanical Advantage, for further information on forces in pulley systems).

The amount of cord needed for rigging depends entirely on the system preferred. Cord length and options for configuring harness and foot ascenders are addressed in chapter 3. Whatever the material, cordage should be inspected often and retired regularly.

Mechanical Ascenders

Mechanical ascenders are metal devices that can be quickly attached to and removed from the rope. A toothed cam (which pivots on the ascender's frame) clamps on to the rope and prevents the rope from moving when the ascender is loaded. When the ascender is slid in the opposite direction, the cam opens, allowing the ascender to slide smoothly along the rope. The rope is prevented from slipping out of the ascender by a safety catch.

A toothed cam usually provides sufficient grip on the rope. In icy conditions, however, the spaces between the teeth may fill up with ice and cause the rope to slip through the ascender. This problem can be alleviated by snapping the cam back and forth a couple of times to remove the ice. Contrary to popular opinion, a toothed cam will not damage the rope when used properly.

Mechanical ascenders are made with or without handles. Handled ascenders are invaluable for rigging, especially in adverse conditions. A handled ascender can be attached to, removed from, and manipulated on the rope with one hand and even with gloves on. Not all handled ascenders will accommodate a mittened hand, so if you plan on wearing mittens select a model with a wide frame, such as the Ushba or CMI expedition ascender. Left- and right-handed versions are available. Figure 2-9 illustrates several different models.

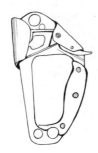

Figure 2-9. Mechanical ascenders, left to right, Ushba, CMI Expedition, Petzl, Jumar.

Mechanical ascenders are designed *for use under body weight only* and should never be used:

- at points in rescue systems where mechanical advantage is multiplied;
- when the potential exists for severe shock loading.

What then, is the best choice for rigging, a set of mechanical ascenders or prusik knots? For many, this decision is reduced to economics. Mechanical ascenders are expensive and heavier, but slide more easily on the rope, have a handle to grip, and can be readily taken from the rope and repositioned at the lip of a crevasse or around anchor points in fixed lines. On the other hand, prusik knots are less expensive and lighter, but take longer to attach to the rope and make ascending somewhat difficult; it can be hard to break the knot repeatedly while ascending a rope with mittens on, and even harder to negotiate the lip of the crevasse if the rope has sliced deeply into the snow. Whatever you choose, bear in mind that knots are stronger than mechanical ascenders and must be used wherever forces are multiplied in a rescue system.

In short, ascenders are worth every ounce where crevasses are large and there is a strong likelihood of falling into one, such as on an Alaskan glacier. When traveling on a smaller glacier with fewer and less ominous crevasses, or with more than one rope team, rigging with prusik knots is reasonable. If it's impossible for a fallen climber to ascend out of a crevasse after a fall (e.g., due to injury, fatigue, slicing of the rope through the lip), the other climbers can team together and provide a quick rescue.

Using one ascender and one prusik knot provides the best of both worlds: reasonable cost and weight, less time needed to rig for travel, and better efficiency when ascending the rope after a crevasse fall.

Mini Ascenders

Two ascending devices that deserve mention due to their lightweight, compact designs are Wild Country's Ropeman Mark II and the Petzl Tibloc ascender (Fig. 2-10). The Ropeman Mark II is a redesigned version of the original Ropeman, and is much better suited for mountaineering than is the original. The most notable improvement has been to the cam, where conical pins have replaced ridges as a means of gripping the rope. This provides a more reliable gripping action in icy conditions and improves the ability of the device to work effectively on smaller-diameter ropes (8.5 to 11 mm.).

The Tibloc also relies on conical pins to grip the rope; however, the pins are housed in the frame of the device, not on a movable cam. An advantage to this design is that there are no moving parts or pins that could fail under load. It's also very light and compact. The Tibloc is also easier to place onto, and remove from the rope than the Ropeman.

Each device slides up (or along) the rope fairly easily; however, neither device is easy to manipulate back down a larger-diameter rope. The pins tend to catch in the rope's sheath. If you plan on rigging with either the Tibloc or the Ropeman, select a smaller-diameter rope (9 mm or less) and practice ascending up and down the rope. Although each of these unique devices can be a versatile replacement for a prusik, a handled ascender is still the best choice for the serious glacier traveler. See chapter 3 for a description of how to rig these devices for glacier travel.

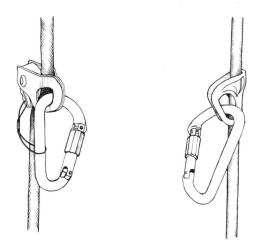

Wild Country Ropeman Mark II   Petzl Tibloc

Figure 2-10. Mini ascenders.

PULLEYS

Pulleys can be invaluable during a rescue, as they significantly reduce the amount of friction in any system incorporating mechanical advantage. For example, a 3:1 (z-pulley) system without pulleys has so much friction that the mechanical advantage is reduced to about 2:1. Each rope team member should carry at least one rescue pulley in an accessible location.

Many brands and models are available (Fig. 2-11). Lightweight (2 oz. to 4 oz.) pulleys usually are inexpensive and well suited for hauling a climber out of a crevasse. Because the side plates are usually constructed from aluminum and the sheaves are usually made from plastic, lightweight pulleys are not designed for heavy rescue loads (e.g., multiple climbers), or for long, continual hauling.

Figure 2-11. Lightweight rescue pulleys,
left to right, REI pulley, CMI pulley, a prusik-minding pulley, a pulley wheel.

Two specialized pulleys are worth mentioning: the prusik-minding pulley and the pulley wheel. The prusik-minding pulley is designed to block a friction knot, making it particularly useful at the anchor during a 3:1 (z-pulley) rescue. The knot does not have to be monitored at the pulley, as it might otherwise have to when a pulley with a wider side plate span is used.

The pulley wheel is simply a nylon wheel that is clipped onto an oval carabiner. Although it's inexpensive and very lightweight (10 g), the rope tends to slip off the wheel during hauling. When a pulley is needed, this *is not* the one to rely on.

CLOTHING

The fundamentals of dressing for glacier travel are the same as for all alpine travel: layers. Start with a layer of soft wicking material, which transports moisture away from the skin and creates a comfort barrier between the skin and outer layer(s). Follow this with one or more insulating layers of wool, synthetic, or down clothing, depending on conditions. The final layer is a waterproof shell to protect the other layers from the elements. Cotton should be avoided at all costs, since it absorbs and holds water and loses most of its insulating value when wet.

Glacier travel does impose one important constraint with respect to clothing: Regardless of surface conditions, *it's essential to dress for the conditions inside a crevasse.* In addition to being prepared for ambient temperatures, which may be far below surface temperatures, a climber in a crevasse must also be prepared to deal with adversities like manipulating an icy rope, dodging snow dislodged from above, and being unable to make major adjustments to clothing.

To keep cool enough for surface travel, yet warm enough to survive in a crevasse, wear clothing that ventilates to provide the widest possible comfort range, such as synthetic clothing, jackets with "pit" zips and wind pants with side zippers. Keep a warm hat and gloves accessible; a tremendous amount of heat can be lost from the head and the hands. Handwear is particularly important, as hands must remain warm enough to manipulate prusiks or ascenders. Don't count on always being able to reach articles of clothing stuffed into a pack pocket, since it's quite possible to end up wedged or partially buried, and unable to get to the pack.

Rigging for Glacier Travel and Rescue

As mountaineering techniques have been refined, safety and rescue systems modified, and equipment redesigned, the number of rigging and rescue options available to the glacier traveler have also increased. Given the multitude of techniques and systems, it's understandable why some climbers have been attracted to the simplified rigging techniques of earlier days, when mountaineers simply tied coils of rope around their waists and went climbing. Although this minimalist approach certainly simplifies the rigging process, it carries a hefty price tag: The risk of serious injury is severe for the climber who falls into a crevasse without the security of a supportive harness and a rigging system that facilitates self-rescue.

There are ways to rig for glacier travel without compromising simplicity. A well-conceived rigging system can be lightweight, easy to set up, and will:

A rope team of three on the Muldrow Glacier, (lower and greater icefalls in the background).
Michael Strong photo

- configure the rope effectively for travel and rescue;
- allow for self- and partner belaying;
- prepare a climber for efficient self-rescue from a crevasse; and
- permit efficient management of a heavy pack or sled, when either or both of these items are utilized.

The cardinal rule of glacier travel is that all rope team members rig for travel before stepping onto the glacier. Patience is hard to come by on a cold morning when everyone is eager to get moving, but keep in mind that the rigging system is an emergency lifeline; getting the rigging in order after a crevasse fall is about as efficient as putting on a seatbelt after a car crash.

CONFIGURING THE ROPE FOR TRAVEL

Prior to roping up, the climbing party must decide how to configure each rope for travel. Some important decisions must be made, such as the number of climbers to put in the rope team, where to place climbers along the rope, the method of attaching each climber to the rope and whether or not to include rescue coils in the configuration scheme.

Spacing and Placement of Climbers Along the Rope

Spacing and placement of climbers along the rope is determined by the nature of the crevasse hazard and the surface conditions of the glacier. Climbers must be far enough apart to reduce the risk of one team member pulling others into a crevasse; the danger of a crevasse fall with multiple climbers increases when spacing is inadequate in relation to the crevasse hazard. On the relatively small glaciers of the Pacific Northwest, 40 feet or so is adequate spacing between climbers. On large Alaskan or Himalayan glaciers where crevasse spans of 50 feet or more are not uncommon, it's recommended that climbers be spaced about 75 feet to 80 feet apart. Keep in mind, however, that the greater the spacing, the more difficult it becomes to keep slack out of the rope while traveling along. Minor "punch-throughs" have turned into full-blown crevasse falls on more than one occasion due to the presence of excessive slack in the rope.

In all cases, it's imperative to space team members equally along the length of the rope; equal spacing ensures that adequate rope is available for rescue during a crevasse fall no matter which team member goes in. The rope team must also balance the need for adequate spacing between team members with the need for mobility. On smaller glaciers with minimal crevasse spans, it's common practice for the team members on each end to collect and carry extra rope in coils (i.e., "end coils"), thereby shortening the rope in order to make travel over and around obstacles faster and more efficient.

Carrying end coils, however, reduces the spacing of climbers along the rope. As stated above, this can present a serious hazard when crevasse spans are very wide.

Availability of Rope for Rescue

Another advantage of carrying end coils is that extra rope is made available for rescue. In some cases (e.g., two-person independent travel) end coils are essential for rescue work. Rescue systems for teams of two and three climbers are described in detail in chapter 6. For the moment, it is enough to emphasize that the dynamics of crevasse rescue must be figured into the rigging equation.

The Number of Climbers on a Rope

For efficiency, speed, and safety, most experienced climbers opt to travel in rope teams of two or three. In some circumstances, a rope team of four or five may be advantageous. The pros and cons of each configuration are discussed below.

The Two-Person Rope Team

The main advantage of two-person travel is speed. In most cases, a two-person rope team will be able to move more quickly and efficiently than any other rope configuration. If mobility is a priority, climbing parties with even numbers are usually better off splitting into rope teams of two.

There are serious disadvantages associated with two-person independent travel. If one person falls into a crevasse and requires extrication, it's very difficult for the remaining team member to place an anchor while in self-arrest; it could be impossible if the slope is steep and icy. Even after the anchor is placed, it is difficult to perform a solo rescue. Realistically, unless a fallen climber can ascend out of the crevasse, the outlook for an independent two-person rope can be grim. Thus, two-person rope teams should be used only if several teams can travel together.

An independent two-person rope team should travel on a 60 meter (196 foot) rope because a long end coil makes more options available for rescue work. The narrow spacing between climbers in Figure 3-1 is inadequate for independent travel on glaciers with large crevasse spans. On glaciers with large crevasse spans, increase your spacing and travel with other rope teams.

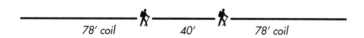

78' coil   40'   78' coil

Figure 3-1. A 196-foot rope configured for two-person independent travel.

The Three-Person Rope Team

A rope team of three is considered the safe minimum for travel by an independent rope team, as two of the three people can carry out any of the rescues described in this book. A three-person rope team, however, usually moves more slowly than a two-person team. For small glaciers, like those found in the continental United States, carry longer end coils to reduce spacing for more efficient maneuvering. On glaciers with wider crevasse spans, increase the spacing between climbers while maintaining adequate rescue rope.

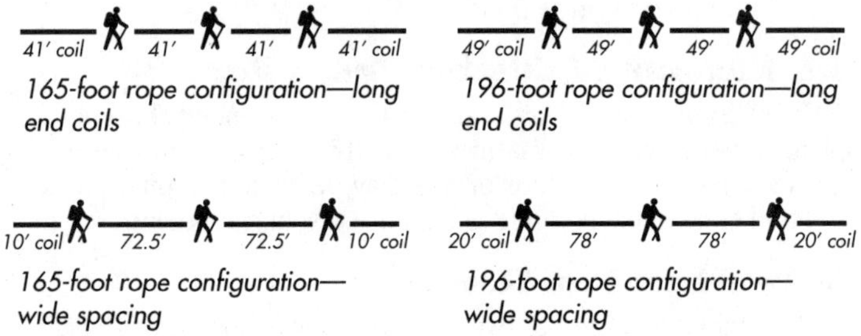

41' coil   41'   41'   41' coil
165-foot rope configuration—long end coils

49' coil   49'   49'   49' coil
196-foot rope configuration—long end coils

10' coil   72.5'   72.5'   10' coil
165-foot rope configuration—wide spacing

20' coil   78'   78'   20' coil
196-foot rope configuration—wide spacing

Figure 3-2. Three-person rope team configurations.

In Figure 3-2 the upper set is for even spacing when traveling on either a 50-meter or 60-meter rope over glaciers with narrow crevasse spans. The lower set is recommended when traveling on either a 50 meter or 60 meter rope on any glacier with wider crevasse spans. Distances between attachment points are shown without knots.

The Four- or Five-Person Rope Team

A party of four or five members can travel on either one or two ropes. Sometimes a party chooses to travel on a single rope to save weight, to place more surface members on the rope to hold a crevasse fall, or perhaps to place weaker members or novices in the middle of the team.

The disadvantages of placing four or five climbers on one rope generally outweigh the advantages. Five climbers traveling on a standard-length rope may end up too close together, increasing the risk of a multiple crevasse fall. Travel through technical terrain is slower, as more time is needed to turn corners, hop crevasses, and travel at a coordinated pace. Rescues can also take longer to execute, as there are more surface members to coordinate. It's usually best to split four or more climbers into two rope teams.

ATTACHING TO THE ROPE

For rock, ice, and alpine climbing, conventional wisdom dictates that you tie directly into the rope in order to eliminate gear that could fail or be misused (i.e., the locking carabiner).

As a general rule, tying directly into the rope is preferable to clipping in for glacier travel as well. There are two situations, however, in which the climber *must* clip into the rope:

• when carrying a heavy pack, and/or
• when pulling a sled.

In either of these situations, any tie-in knot will jam solidly and be almost impossible to untie after a crevasse fall. As explained later in this chapter, a climber who suffers a crevasse fall while encumbered by a sled or a heavy pack must be able to detach from the rope in order to perform a self-rescue.

To attach climbers to the rope, divide the rope into appropriate sections, accounting for equal and adequate spacing, rescue rope, and the number of climbers (as discussed earlier). End climbers have their choice of tying or clipping into the rope while the middle person(s) must clip in. Tie-in and clip-in knots are reviewed in appendix 1.

The *kiwi coil* is a popular *tie-in* method when carrying a light pack, because it allows climbers to easily adjust the spacing between each other, provides readily accessible rescue coils, and adds flexibility to the rigging system. Climbers can easily pick up or drop coils without having to detach from the rope. The coil also serves as an impromptu chest harness.

To rig with a kiwi coil, tie into the end of the rope, coil an agreed upon amount of extra rope over the shoulder, and tie the coil off as shown in Figure 3-3. When tied correctly, the force of a fall is transferred directly and exclusively to the seat harness; the shoulder coil doesn't constrict or sustain any force.

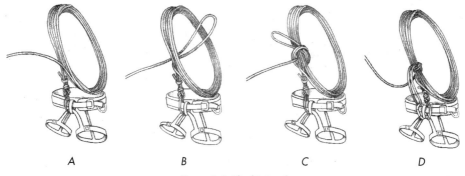

A   B   C   D

Figure 3-3. The kiwi coil.

A second option is to clip into the designated place on the rope and stuff the trailing section of rescue rope into a pack, or coil this section over the shoulder and tie it off with a clove hitch (Fig. 3-4).

Figure 3-4. Rope coil with clove hitch tie-off.

RIGGING WITH PRUSIK KNOTS AND MECHANICAL ASCENDERS

A glacier rig consists of two elements: a seat harness ascender and a foot ascender. The set-up varies slightly depending on whether you use *prusik knots* or *mechanical ascenders* to rig for travel. Rigging with prusik knots is the logical choice for the casual glacier traveler. Climbers who spend a significant amount of time on glaciers may find the added convenience of mechanical ascenders worth the extra weight and expense.

Rigging with Prusik Knots

Of the many friction knots available, the prusik knot is the most popular choice by far. It's easy to tie, and in contrast to other friction knots (e.g., Klemheist, Bachmann) works equally well in both directions and is less prone to working loose over the course of the day. Figures of the various friction knots are provided in appendix 1.

The Seat Harness Prusik

Select a short, 5- to 6-foot section of accessory cord and tie the ends together with a grapevine knot. As explained in chapter 2, the diameter of the cord must be *at least three mm smaller* than the diameter of the climbing rope in order for the prusik knot to solidly grip the rope.

Tie the prusik loop onto the rope with a prusik knot and clip the loop into a locking carabiner in the seat harness. Make sure that the grapevine knot doesn't interfere at the carabiner clip-in point (Fig. 3-5). The length of the loop depends on your reach. When pushed along the rope as far as the loop allows, the prusik knot must remain comfortably within reach.

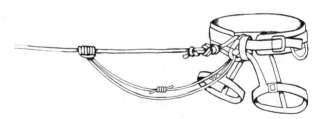

Figure 3-5. Seat harness prusik.

The Foot Prusik

A number of reasonable options exist for constructing a foot prusik, including:
- a single strand of cord with loops tied into each end,
- a single strand foot prusik with a harness tether,
- a long looped sling, or
- the Texas prusik system, which utilizes two foot loops.

Each configuration is presented below; experience and personal preference will determine which one you adopt.

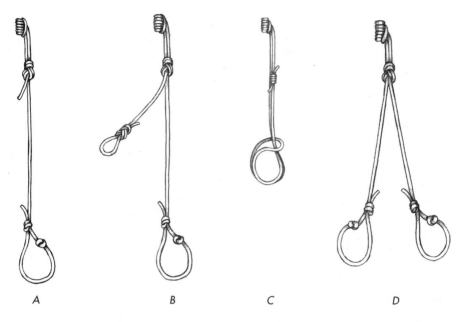

A	B	C	D
Single strand from 9 to 10 feet of cord.	Single strand with a harness tether from approximately 12 feet of cord.	Long looped sling tied from approximately 10 feet of cord.	Texas prusik constructed from approximately 12 to 14 feet of cord.

Figure 3-6. Options for constructing a foot prusik.

- *Single strand foot prusik*—A simple, yet effective foot prusik can be constructed by tying loops into the ends of a 9- to 10-foot strand of accessory cord. One loop (approximately 6 inches long) serves as the prusik knot's attachment to the rope. At the other end, a sliding knot (i.e., one that cinches down such as a grapevine) accommodates the foot (Fig. 3-6A). If you want to add a harness tether to the foot prusik (Fig. 3-6B), a useful adaptation for middle person rigging, you'll need a slightly longer section of cord (approximately 12 feet).

To prevent the knot from cinching down and restricting circulation, add a "blocker knot" inside the foot loop (Fig. 3-7). A half of a double fisherman's with an overhand blocker knot works well, and the loop can be easily adjusted to accommodate crampons or overboots.

- *Long looped sling*—You can tie a longer version of the seat harness prusik from approximately 10 feet of cord (Fig. 3-6C). After a crevasse fall, the free end of the loop is girth-hitched to your boot. The main advantage of this

Figure 3-7. Blocker knot.

method is that the double strand of cord is stronger than any method that has a foot loop tied with a single strand of cord, an important consideration for use in a rescue system.

- *The Texas prusik system*—This provides a foot loop for each leg, allowing better balance while ascending and distributing the workload to both legs (Fig. 3-6D). To construct a Texas prusik, tie a figure-of-eight on a bight into the middle of a 12- to 14-foot piece of cord. This loop serves as the prusik knot's attachment to the rope. Fashion each end into a foot loop as discussed earlier, again placing blocker knots to prevent overtightening.

Regardless of the method used, tie the foot prusik onto the rope and stuff the foot loop(s) into a pocket. It's possible to carry the prusik loop on a gear loop, however, it may be very inconvenient to tie the cord onto the climbing rope after a crevasse fall, especially with gloves on. It's also easy to drop the cord or a glove. It's more convenient to detach this cord from the rope if it's needed for rescue than to attach it to the rope after a fall!

Height and Reach of the Prusiks

Fine tune the length of the seat harness and foot prusiks before heading out onto the glacier. With the foot prusik attached to the rope, the prusik knot should be at waist level with the foot (or feet) flat on the surface of the snow. With the foot fully elevated, the foot prusik should end up slightly lower on the rope than the harness prusik when it's also at full extension, as shown in Figure 3-8. Some fine tuning will invariably be needed to attain this relationship.

Keep in mind that changing the foot attachment method, or even the type of boots may affect the relationship between the two cords. Should the distance between cords change significantly, adjust the length accordingly. It's nearly impossible to adjust the cords while dangling in a crevasse, so take some time to fine tune your ascension system at home or at the local playground. Proper adjustment is critical for efficient self rescue!

Arrangement of the Prusiks on the Rope

Attach the harness prusik furthest along the rope (Fig. 3-9). This prusik can then be utilized as a self-belay, or as a belay for a rope partner without the interference of the foot prusik. Belaying with the harness prusik is described in chapter 4.

Figure 3-8. Correct adjustment of harness and foot prusiks. When using a foot prusik that incorporates a harness tether, make sure that the harness tether is long enough to allow unrestricted movement of the foot prusik up the rope.

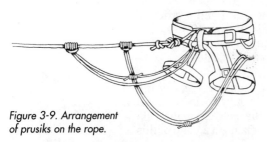

Figure 3-9. Arrangement of prusiks on the rope.

The Middle Person

Rigging for the middle person is slightly more complex as this person will probably be called on to belay leading and trailing team members with the harness prusik when entering or leaving safe zones. The middle person must also be prepared to ascend either rope after a crevasse fall. For efficiency during travel, and safety while dangling in a crevasse, it's ideal for the middle person to be rigged with a harness and foot prusik on the leading and trailing ropes. Not quite as good, but still acceptable, is a rigging system that utilizes two harness prusiks and one foot prusik, as shown in Figure 3-10.

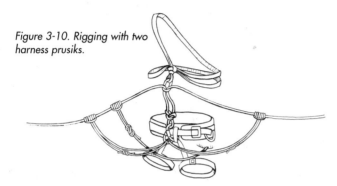

Figure 3-10. Rigging with two harness prusiks.

With this set-up the middle person is ready to belay leading and trailing members when called upon, and is prepared to ascend either of the two ropes after a fall. There's a 50-50 chance that the foot prusik is rigged on the correct line. If not, the middle person will have to retie the foot prusik onto the correct rope in order to ascend. Aside from an unpleasant delay in self-rescue, the main drawback to this arrangement is that the climber could drop a prusik cord while retying it, making a surface rescue necessary if the climber has no spare cord.

Another option is to rig with a harness prusik on one rope and a foot prusik (with a harness tether) on the other(Fig. 3-11). The main advantage of this option is that the climber can rig a harness tether on both ropes with one less prusik cord than is required in the rigging option shown in Figure 3-10.

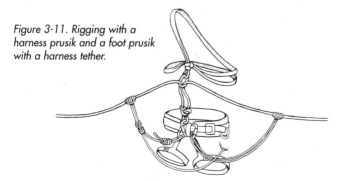

Figure 3-11. Rigging with a harness prusik and a foot prusik with a harness tether.

Rigging with Mechanical Ascenders

Although they are heavier than prusik cords, mechanical ascenders simplify the rigging process and make travel and rescue easier and more efficient. The basic ascension system remains the same, requiring a harness and a foot loop. Attach a short tether to each ascender and clip the tethers to the seat harness carabiner. Tie a foot loop to the foot ascender and stuff the loop into a pocket. As shown in Figure 3-12, the foot ascender has two tethers. The harness tether on the foot ascender is a critical addition to the rigging set-up, as it prevents the foot ascender from becoming lost should you drop the ascender when attaching it to the rope during self-rescue.

Make sure that the seat harness tether on the foot ascender is long enough to permit full extension of the foot ascender up the rope. In this fully extended position, the tether should have a little slack. The same principles for length (or reach), that apply to prusik knots also apply when using ascenders. Once again, practice is necessary.

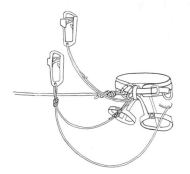

Figure 3-12. Rigging with ascenders.

Clip each ascender to a shoulder sling or to a gear loop on the harness, keeping them off the rope during travel. If an ascender is on the rope while traveling, it could slide into a position where it holds the full force of a crevasse fall, risking damage to the rope and perhaps facial injury if you're pulled into the snow during a fall by a team member.

Rigging with ascenders is particularly advantageous for the middle person in a rope team, as it eliminates the need for dual harness and foot prusiks for belaying and self-rescue.

Rigging with an Ascender and a Prusik Cord

Many climbers are deterred by the expense and added weight of mechanical ascenders despite their convenience. A good compromise is to use a single ascender and a prusik cord.

Attach the ascender to the seat harness. In this position the ascender can be quickly clipped past an embedded rope, around anchor points, or onto another team's rope in order to provide a belay. Tie the foot prusik onto the rope and stuff the cord into a pocket.

This arrangement is particularly useful for the middle person in a rope team, as it avoids the need for two harness prusiks; the harness ascender can be quickly placed onto the leading and/or following ropes during belaying and self-rescue.

Rigging a Ropeman or Tibloc Ascender

Either of these ascending devices can be used in place of a harness or foot prusik. Adjust for length as you would any other ascending device. Since both the Ropeman and Tibloc are held in place by a carabiner, it takes longer to place them onto, and remove them from the rope than a handled ascender.

As a result, you may find it more convenient to leave them on the rope during travel. Remember to travel with plenty of slack in the harness ascender should you decide in favor of this option. Any forceful fall should be held by the rope's attachment to the harness, not the sharp teeth of an ascender.

A daisy chain greatly facilitates the rigging process. Multiple clip points save time when rigging for reach. The daisy chain also provides a secure, adjustable attachment to

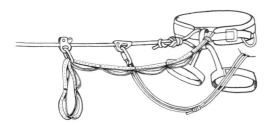

Figure 3-13. Rigging a Tibloc or Ropeman.

an anchor during rescue work (once the ascending device is removed from the rope; see Fig. 3-13).

RIGGING WITH A HEAVY PACK

The rigging system described in the previous section is designed for climbers carrying light summit packs. When traveling on a glacier with a heavy (i.e., backpacking weight) pack, there are several important modifications you should make to the rigging system.

First: Clip into the rope rather than tying in. The forces exerted in a crevasse fall with a heavy pack on will solidly jam any tie-in knot, making it impossible to untie from the rope, especially with mittens on, or cold hands. If you cannot untie from the rope, you will be forced to ascend with at least a portion of the pack's weight, a torturous and perhaps impossible task. The best solution is to unclip from the rope, and leave the pack dangling securely below while ascending to safety. Several options for attaching the pack are described and diagrammed below.

Second: Attach two locking carabiners to the seat harness: one for the harness prusik and one for the climbing rope. This arrangement creates two independent attachment systems, allowing you to unclip from the rope without compromising the security of the seat harness prusik. The possibility of trapping the rope behind the prusik cord is also avoided, a real possibility if the rope and prusik cord are attached to the same locking carabiner.

Third: The pack itself must be attached to the rope during travel, so that it's possible to take it off and leave it dangling on the rope after a crevasse fall. The following sections discuss several rigging options.

The Pack Prusik and Tether

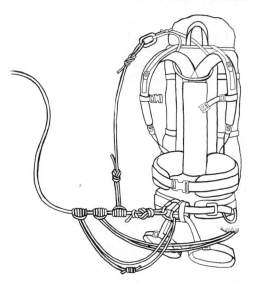

Attach a pack prusik to the climbing rope. It must be the innermost prusik knot on the rope. In this position, the pack prusik does not obstruct the foot or harness prusiks during self-rescue. Clip the pack prusik to a tether attached to the pack.

There are two significant advantages of using a pack prusik. Once you have ascended the rope a little after a fall (just far enough for slack to develop in the rope's attachment to the seat harness), the pack prusik can then be slid up, and the pack taken off. You can now detach from the rope's clip-in point without having to struggle with the pack's weight. Second, if the pack prusik has been correctly adjusted ahead of time, the pack will be right beside you, making an extra clothing layer, mittens, a hat, or additional gear readily available. Figure 3-14 illustrates the use of a pack prusik and tether.

Figure 3-14. A pack prusik and tether.

Pack Tether Clipped to the Clip-in Knot

In this set-up, the pack tether is attached to the clip-in loop (Fig. 3-15). Use a separate locking carabiner for this purpose. Do not clip the pack tether to the seat harness carabiner, as the weight of the pack will be placed directly on the seat harness when the pack is taken off, making it necessary to ascend with the full weight of the pack.

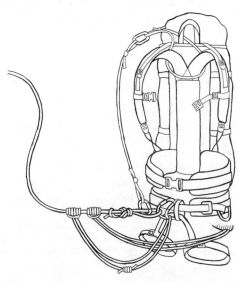

Figure 3-15. A pack tether on the loop formed by the clip-in knot.

Pack Tethered with the Rope End

You can also use the rope end as a tether. Although this option eliminates the need for a separate sling, this attachment method (Fig. 3-16) does not allow you the option of configuring rescue coils into the end of the rope.

For any of the above methods, the pack is hauled up as the last step in the rescue process. An additional advantage of leaving the pack on the rope below is that the pack's weight tensions the rope, making it much easier for the climber to ascend.

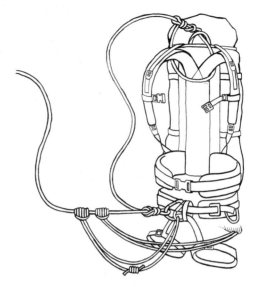

Figure 3-16. A pack tethered with the end of the rope.

Pack Tether Clipped to the Climbing Rope

Yet another option is to attach a tether to the pack and clip the tether to the climbing rope during travel, as shown in Figure 3-17. After a crevasse fall do not detach yourself from the rope; leave the pack hanging below you, sliding on the bight of rope that develops as you ascend.

Although ascending with a light pack sliding on the rope below you is feasible, rigging this way with a heavy pack is unwise, as about one-half of the pack's weight must be lifted with every step. There are other disadvantages to using this method: Access to the pack compartments is not possible, placing an extra layer, mittens or a hat out of reach. The pack may also wedge into the lip of the crevasse during ascent, preventing upward movement. This is a concern after a short fall, for the pack is immediately below the climber.

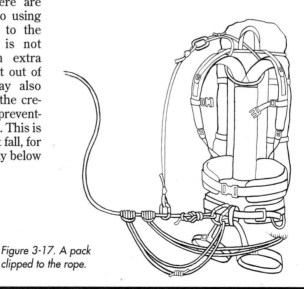

Figure 3-17. A pack clipped to the rope.

Which Rigging Option to Choose?

All of the options described have advantages and disadvantages. Pack weight and personal choice dictate how to rig. With a very heavy pack, use a pack prusik so the pack can be removed before you need to fiddle with the rope's attachment to the seat harness. This method is also advantageous in very cold weather when you may need to access a pack compartment for extra clothing layers. The pack prusik is the only rigging option that makes the pack easily accessible.

If the pack is lighter and you do not need immediate access to the pack after a fall, consider rigging with the pack tether clipped to the clip-in knot. It's fast and simple to rig, and, held by the clip-in loop, the pack tether attachment stays out of the way during travel. During a crevasse fall, the attachment can either be left where it is or, if you feel up to hauling the pack as you ascend, can easily be clipped to the rope.

Whatever method you choose for attaching the pack to the rope, be sure that the tether is firmly attached to the pack. Never attach a tether to a heavy pack using only the pack's hang loop or to a single shoulder strap. A better arrangement is to pass the tether through both shoulder straps or, at least, through a shoulder strap and the hang loop. This arrangement also keeps the pack hanging upright.

As described in chapter 2, it's absolutely essential to wear a chest harness while carrying a heavy pack. The risk of serious injury can be reduced with proper use of a chest harness.

RIGGING CONSIDERATIONS FOR SLED USE

On longer trips many climbers use sleds to move loads up the glacier. There are definite advantages to sled use: More weight can be hauled with a sled than can be easily carried by pack, and the weight is distributed over a larger surface area during travel, reducing the load placed on snowbridges. On the negative side, a sled is cumbersome and difficult to manage on sidehills and when maneuvering in steeper, more heavily crevassed terrain. A sled may also have to be carried at times, making the overall load heavier.

Sleds with rigid poles provide the most control. A rigid pole system keeps the sled at a fixed distance, which is helpful for control on downhills. The poles can also be crossed, making it easier to manage the sled while traversing a slope. Rotating the hips downhill while traversing points the sled uphill, allowing the sled to track effectively. Gear can also be packed relatively high with less possibility of the sled rolling over on traverses. A rigid pole system, however, provides a jerky ride, and there's a noticeable push from behind on steeper slopes.

Sled travel is by no means a one-person effort, especially if cord or slings are used to pull the sled. In the absence of a rigid pole system, the trailing rope team member becomes very active in controlling the sled on sidehills, downhills, and around crevasses and other obstacles. This person can greatly facilitate progress by keeping the sled on track and upright and can provide immediate aid in emergencies.

It may be even more challenging to pull a drag bag. No more than a slippery, durable, waterproof bag into which gear is sealed, the drag bag lacks form and has a tendency to roll, or swing downhill on the slightest sidehill. Drag bags are lighter than sleds, however, and are ideally suited to travel over wide, relatively flat well consolidated glacial surfaces.

A sled should *never* be pulled by the last person on a rope team because it must be caught from behind during a crevasse fall. Serious injury is almost certain should a sled land on the fallen climber.

Rigging a Sled

Sled Prusik

One option for rigging the sled is with a prusik knot (Fig. 3-18). Attach a short loop of accessory cord to the trailing rope with a prusik knot at a point behind the sled. Clip the cord to a *very strong* attachment point on the rear of the sled. During a fall, the prusik knot grips the rope and holds the sled in place.

Make sure the prusik knot will grip the rope securely when loaded, and is not tightened on the rope so far toward the trailing rope team member that a loop of slack develops between the prusik knot and the sled-puller's clip-in point, causing the knot (rather than the climbing rope) to take the full force of a fall by the trailing climber. Some fine tuning is likely to be required to achieve the correct placement of the prusik knot on the rope. Check this knot often over the course of a day, ensuring that it is tight and correctly positioned.

Figure 3-18. Rigging a sled with a prusik loop.

Rigging with a Butterfly Knot

Another option is to attach the sled to a butterfly knot (see appendix 1) tied into the rope, as shown in Figure 3-19. Unlike the prusik, the butterfly knot cannot slip and therefore does not have to be monitored during travel. It does, however, require a little more initial work to get the tension just right.

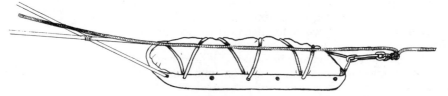

Figure 3-19. Rigging a sled with a butterfly knot.

Attaching with Clove Hitches

You can also attach both the front and rear ends of the sled to the rope with clove hitches (see appendix 1), as shown in Figure 3-20. Again, sled attachment points must be strong, and the knots adjusted such that once tied, there is no slack between them.

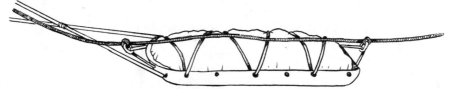

Figure 3-20. Rigging a sled with clove hitches.

The advantage of rigging with clove hitches is that the person behind can pull on the rope (on downhills, sidehills, or maneuvering around obstacles) without altering the tension in any section of the rope. A disadvantage is that a climber must ascend past two rope-to-sled attachment points rather than one sled prusik after a fall.

When pulling a sled (Fig. 3-21):

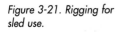
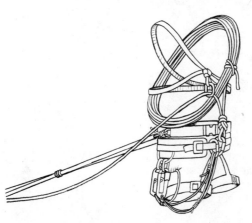

Figure 3-21. Rigging for sled use.

- Use an ascending system that makes it easy to bypass the sled on the way up the rope. Mechanical ascenders are best, since they can be taken off the rope and quickly re-attached past a prusik knot or clove hitches. At the very least, use one mechanical ascender.

- Attach the harness ascender to a locking seat harness carabiner and clip the climbing rope into a separate locking carabiner, as described in the preceding section on rigging with a heavy pack. After a fall, detachment from the climbing rope will be necessary in order to ascend past the sled; using separate carabiners for rope and seat ascender attachment points avoids the possibility of detaching completely from the rope.

THE BUDDY SYSTEM

Let's face it, everyone makes mistakes in rigging. Fatigue, dehydration, poor lighting, and numb fingers virtually ensure that at some point somebody in the climbing group will forget to attach an ascender, lock a carabiner, or mis-tie a knot. Such mistakes are more likely to be noticed if the rope team makes a habit of checking each other's rigging before setting out across the glacier. Give each other a quick once over, checking to make sure that harnesses are worn correctly with buckles doubled back, tie-in or clip-in knots are attached correctly, carabiners are locked and not cross-loaded, ascenders are properly attached, and adequate rescue gear is carried by each team member. It takes just a moment and is well worth the time. Be consistent in all checks so that no item goes uninspected.

It should be emphasized that the buddy system is not something meant only for novices. Many experienced climbers use it religiously, having learned that a simple oversight can have serious consequences for all members of the rope team.

RESCUE GEAR

In addition to the gear required for rigging, each person should carry the following items:

- one anchor for the surface conditions likely to be encountered (picket, fluke, ice screw, firn tube). When traveling over a variety of surface conditions, you may have to carry more than one kind of anchor.
- one sling long enough to construct a tension release mechanism (a 16- to 20-foot cordelette is ideal)
- one short sling (to attach to the anchor)
- two nonlocking carabiners
- a rappel device (or enough carabiners to rappel), or a pear-shaped carabiner in the harness from which to rappel with a Müenter hitch
- a rescue pulley (or two more carabiners)

Two clmbers test a self-equalized anchor backed up by a bollard. Diller Glacier, Oregon.
Michael Strong photo

ANCHORS

In addition to forming the foundation for crevasse rescue systems, anchors provide security to rope team members on exposed terrain. For example, the leader may place a series of anchor points while the team traverses a steep slope above a cliff band, forming a running belay. Or the team may decide to place a fixed belay anchor to provide security for a tenuous snowbridge crossing. Whatever the case, it's essential that every rope team member have a solid understanding of how to place individual anchors, identify where they're most likely to be needed, and know how to combine single anchors into anchor systems.

The basic principle of an anchor system is simple: Create two or more anchor points by ramming, burying, or screwing suitable objects in the snow or ice, then tie them all together in such a way that the forces generated by the load are evenly distributed between them. In practice, creating a reliable anchor system can be challenging. The number of anchor points needed, the type of anchors to use, and how they are joined into an anchor system all vary with snow conditions and terrain. This chapter presents the fundamentals of anchor system construction with an in-depth look at the various options for creating anchor points and discusses ways of joining these points into well-configured anchor systems.

ANCHOR POINTS

Individual anchor points are the building blocks of an anchor system; if the anchor points are weak, the anchor system will probably fail. There are many different types of snow and ice anchors: snow flukes, pickets, deadmen, firn tubes, ice screws, and bollards, each designed for a different type of surface condition. The key to setting solid anchors is choosing anchor pieces that are appropriate for the surface consistency and placing them properly. The following paragraphs discuss various forms of snow protection in detail.

Anchors for Soft Snow

Snow Flukes

Snow flukes are large metal plates that are set into the snow perpendicular to the anticipated direction of force. When placed properly, a fluke will dive even farther into the snow when subjected to load, providing a solid anchor placement. Flukes are designed primarily for snow enough soft that they can be easily trenched or driven in. The snow must be dense enough, however, to prevent movement of the fluke once it's placed. When snow conditions are very soft (e.g., light powder) it's usually necessary to boot pack the snow before placing the fluke.

Flukes come in different sizes. A large fluke will provide better holding power but will be harder to place in firm snow. Flukes vary widely in design as well. Older flukes are often just flat plates; more modern designs are bent in the middle (like an open book), which allows the fluke to automatically reposition itself when one side of the fluke takes more force. Modern flukes are frequently perforated to reduce weight as well. Some designs incorporate an anvil of harder alloy along the top edge to prevent the top surface from being damaged when the fluke is pounded into very firm snow.

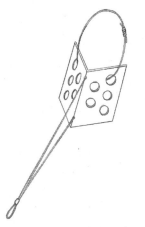

Figure 4-1. Snow fluke with retrieval cord.

Regardless of differences in size and plate design, all flukes will have a swaged cable passing through two vertically aligned holes in the plate surface. The upper cable section is longer than the lower one, placing the fluke at an angle of 30 to 40 degrees from the perpendicular when the cables are stretched out horizontally. An optional retrieval cord may be added to the top of the fluke to ease removal (Fig. 4-1).

To place a fluke, prepare the site, either by scraping away loose surface snow to reach firm snow, or stirring up and then packing down unconsolidated snow. If the snow surface is firm and compact already, it may require no further preparation. If you discover an ice layer beneath the snow surface do not place a fluke because the fluke will deflect off the ice layer when it's loaded. Depending on the hardness and thickness of the ice layer, a picket or ice screw will provide more secure protection in this situation.

Next, cut a trench deep enough to contain the fluke below the surface. Make sure that the slot is cut and the fluke placed at the correct angle: 30 to 40 degrees backward from a perpendicular orientation to the slope (Fig. 4-2). The softer the snow, the deeper the trench. Let snow consistency serve as a guide, keeping in mind that it's the mass of snow in front of the fluke that determines the security of fluke placement. Cut a narrow slot for the fluke cables with the axe pick, in line with the direction of pull. The slot must be deep enough to prevent the cables from riding up and pulling the fluke in an upward direction. This is especially important in firm snow.

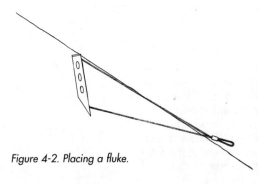

Figure 4-2. Placing a fluke.

Set the fluke by placing it in the trench and giving the cable a solid tug. When set properly, the tension will be equal on each cable section, with the top cable aligned parallel to the surface of the slope. Give the fluke a slightly harder tug and observe the motion of the fluke. If all is well, the fluke will dive downward into the snow under load. If the fluke pulls out, it's either because it wasn't placed properly or it was set in poorly consolidated snow. Correct any problems, then pack snow back into the trench to hold the fluke firmly in place. Figures 4-3 and 4-4 illustrate common problems with fluke placement.

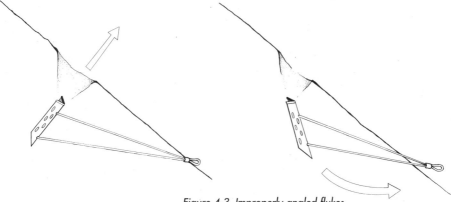

Figure 4-3. Improperly angled flukes.

Placement angle too shallow. When a fluke is not angled back far enough, it slaps against the lower wall of the trench and is at risk of pulling up and out. An ice layer may also prevent the fluke from setting properly, even if it was initially placed at the correct angle.

Placement angle too steep. When a fluke is angled back too far, it can "skate" and eventually pull out, especially if it is placed just above an ice layer.

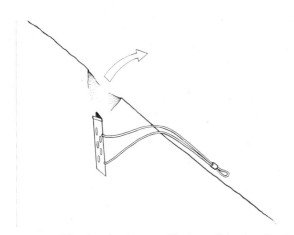

Figure 4-4. Fluke placed without a cable slot. A fluke placed without a cable slot is at great risk of pulling up and out. Cut slots for any buried anchor that has a section of cable or webbing attached to it.

Some climbers prefer to drive flukes into the snow rather than bury them. Though this process is faster, it's more difficult to assess the quality of the placement, and the top of the fluke may be damaged over time. When driving a fluke in, remember to carve a trench for the cables, just as when burying the fluke. Finally, keep in mind that flukes are unidirectional anchors, able only to resist forces perpendicular to their placement.

Deadman Anchors

There are times, usually in early season or after a heavy snowfall, when surface snow is so loose and powdery that flukes just won't work; an anchor with greater surface area is needed. Fortunately, the glacier traveler is usually well equipped with any number of items that can be pressed into service as deadman anchors. Packs, large stuffsacks filled with snow, and skis work very well (Fig. 4-5).

Site preparation is straightforward; simply bury a suitable item sideways, girth-hitch it at its center of mass with a long sling, and cut a slot for the sling. Cover the entire placement with snow and boot pack the area firmly. The tail end of the sling should remain on the surface, ready for use. Though these improvised placements may require substantial effort, it's comforting to know that a very strong anchor can be created in even the poorest of conditions.

Figure 4-5. An improvised anchor—a stuff sack filled with snow.

A picket (or an axe) may also be buried sideways as a deadman (Fig. 4-6). In this orientation, the picket has as much, if not more, surface area than an average-sized fluke, providing a very solid anchor.

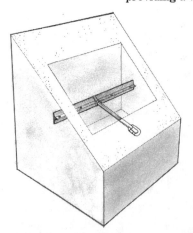
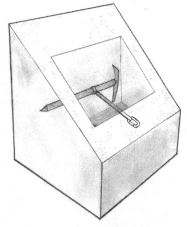

Figure 4-6. A picket and an axe placed in deadman orientation. Note: When placing the axe as a deadman, girth-hitch the center of mass (not the middle) of the axe.

Anchors for Firm Snow

Pickets

Pickets are 2- to 4-foot extruded aluminum stakes designed to be driven into very firm snow. Some pickets are V-shaped in cross-section with a single carabiner hole near the top; more modern designs are T-shaped in cross-section and incorporate multiple carabiner holes along their length. Either design is acceptable when placed properly, although the increased rigidity and surface area of modern T-shaped pickets provides somewhat greater holding power than the older V-shaped design.

To place a picket, angle it back approximately 30 degrees from a perpendicular orientation to the slope and pound it in, preferably with an ice hammer, although an adze will work in softer snow. If the snow is soft enough to plunge the picket in by hand, it's too soft for picket placement; use a snow fluke or deadman anchor. After pounding the picket completely in, clip a carabiner to the hole, and it's ready for use. If a solid layer prevents the picket from going in all the way, tie it off at the surface with a runner (to avoid leverage; Fig. 4-7).

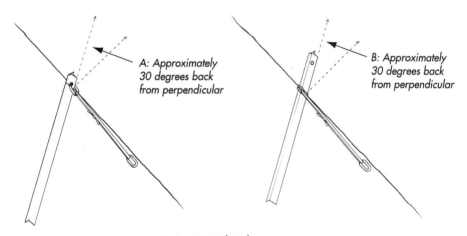

A: Approximately 30 degrees back from perpendicular

B: Approximately 30 degrees back from perpendicular

Figure 4-7. Picket placement.

An ice axe can also be used as a picket, provided that it's strong enough. As with factory-made pickets, tilt the axe back approximately 30 degrees from perpendicular to the load (Fig. 4-8).

Figure 4-8. Ice axe placed as a picket.

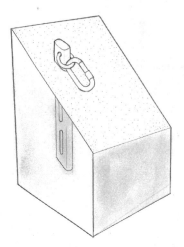

Firn Tubes

When the snow is too hard for pickets and too soft for ice screws, nothing works better than a firn tube. A hammer is needed to drive the tube in. The same considerations for placing pickets apply to firn tubes (Fig. 4-9).

Ice Anchors

Ice Screws

Ice screws are necessary whenever the ice is exposed, or the snowpack overlying the glacier's ice surface is too thin to effectively hold flukes, pickets, or deadmen. Be sure that it's ice, and not just very firm snow before selecting ice screws as protection. Longer, tubular ice screws hold better than shorter screws or the pound-in, screw-out designs in relatively soft glacier ice.

Figure 4-9. A firn tube.

Prepare the site for screw placement by scraping or cutting away any soft or brittle layers. When solid ice is reached, angle the screw back approximately 15 degrees from perpendicular to the load (Fig. 4-10). Next, use the pick of the axe to chop a small starter hole in the middle of the platform. Place the screw, sinking it all the way in; the carabiner hole should end up facing the load. If the ice is very hard (or the screw dull) the pick of the axe may be needed to help turn the screw. Hook the pick through the carabiner hole in the screw and turn gently. Be careful not to bend the axe pick sideways or it may break.

Screw placements tend to melt out very quickly in warmer temperatures, as the metal of the screw conducts heat down

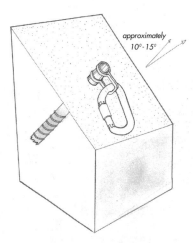

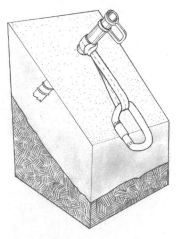

Figure 4-10. Ice screw placements. If a screw cannot be placed to the hilt, tie it off with a piece of webbing to reduce leverage.

into the ice. Pressure on a screw from the weight of a load can also melt the ice supporting the loaded side of the screw. In either case, the result can be a dangerously loose screw. Though melt-out can be slowed by covering the placement with a mound of snow, it's important to check the placements frequently. For rescue purposes, it's imperative to use more than one ice screw.

Bollards—Anchors for Ice or Snow

When a stout back-up anchor is needed for an ice screw, an ice bollard is an ideal choice. Bollards can also be excellent primary anchors, whether in ice or snow. The major drawback of bollards is that they take a good deal of time and effort to construct.

In essence, a bollard is nothing more than a large horn of ice or snow that is slung with a length of webbing (Fig. 4-11). The appropriate size for a bollard depends on the consistency of the surface. In hard ice, a bollard a foot or so wide and several inches deep will hold a great deal of force; in soft snow, a bollard may need to be upwards of 5 feet in diameter and more than a foot deep in order to be useful.

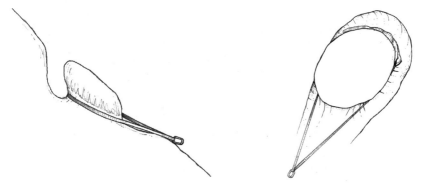

Figure 4-11. Side and top views of a bollard. Note: Make sure the inside angle of the sling is less than 90 degrees.

To construct a bollard, trace a line in the snow or ice describing the desired shape and size of the bollard. The overall shape (viewed from above) should be like a teardrop, with the point aimed in the direction of anticipated force. Excavate a trench along the line traced in the snow, and dig deep enough to create a substantial (tear-shaped) pillar of snow or ice. Before slinging the bollard, undercut its back and side lips in order to prevent the sling from sliding over the top of the bollard under load (Fig. 4-11).

When building a bollard in soft snow, it is also wise to pad the back lip with an Ensolite pad, a pack, or a bunched-up piece of tubular webbing to help reduce the tendency of the sling to cut through the bollard. Pickets, ice axes, or other similarly shaped items can also be placed vertically in the back of the bollard to strengthen it.

Finally, sling the bollard. Be sure the sling is long enough so that the angle between the two legs of the sling is less than 90 degrees. If the bollard is symmetrical and well-constructed, the force of the load should be evenly distributed around the bollard's back side.

ANCHOR SYSTEMS

A solid anchor system is the foundation for any technical rescue. Although there are situations in which a single anchor placement may be adequate (e.g., when setting running belays), the forces involved in crevasse rescue make a multipoint anchor absolutely imperative. The number of anchor points joined to construct an anchor system will vary with snow conditions and the team's resources. The bare minimum for crevasse rescue is one anchor system constructed from two strong placements. In poor snow conditions it may be necessary to back up one anchor system with another, using up to four anchor points in all.

Although it is often convenient to initially support a fallen climber's weight on one well-placed anchor, expansion to a multipoint anchor system should remain a top priority. Never begin hauling the climber (i.e., applying mechanical advantage) until at least two anchor points have been joined to create a multipoint anchor. When hauling begins, the force on the anchor system may be several times the fallen climber's weight. Failure of the anchor system in midrescue is perhaps the worst catastrophe that can befall a rope team. If there's any reason to doubt the integrity of the anchor system, stop and reinforce it!

Three methods are commonly used to combine anchor points into an anchor system. These are shown in Figures 4-12 through 4-15.

Self-Equalizing Anchor System

Imagine an anchor system consisting of two anchor points, with a separate sling running from each point to a carabiner that holds the load. If one sling is even slightly longer than the other, the entire weight of the load will be carried by the anchor point with the shorter sling; if that placement fails, the entire load will suddenly come onto the second anchor point, shock-loading it. Obviously, it would be better to divide the load between the two placements so that each anchor point never has to hold more than a portion of the full load. This principle, known as *equalization,* is a golden rule of anchor system construction.

One way to ensure that the load is shared by all anchor components is to construct a *self-equalizing* anchor system, in which two (or more) anchor points are joined with a sling using a sliding knot. Begin by clipping the sling into each anchor point so that a large loop is formed (Fig. 4-12A). Take the top strand of the sling (the one between the anchor points) and twist a loop into it (Fig. 4-12B). Clip the loop to the bottom strand with a carabiner (Fig. 4-12C). A sliding knot is formed. If the load moves to one side or the other, the sliding knot compensates, always equalizing the load on the anchor points.

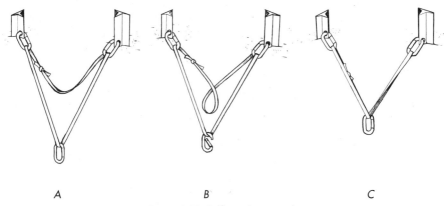

| A | B | C |

Figure 4-12. Self-equalizing anchor system.

Several points about this anchor system deserve special emphasis. First, the inner angle between the "legs" of the sling should be less than 90 degrees. As the angle grows above 90 degrees, the force that each anchor point is subjected to grows as well. At 120 degrees, each anchor point is subjected to the full load. The easiest way to reduce the inner angle is to simply use a longer sling.

Second, a drawback of the sliding knot is that the sling is not redundant. If the sling breaks, the anchor will fail. Also, if one of the anchor points fails, the load will fall some distance (about the length of the sling) and shock-load the remaining anchor point, possibly causing complete anchor failure. For these reasons, it's safest to incorporate redundancy into the system by either tying each leg of the sling off with an overhand knot (Fig. 4-13) or attaching a back-up sling to one of the anchor points.

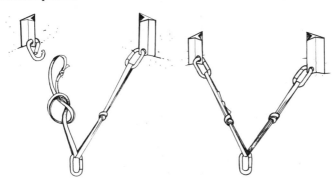

Figure 4-13. Tying the sling off for redundancy.

Position Equalized Anchor

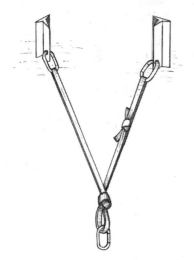

A *position equalized* anchor is based on the same concepts as the self-equalizing system just described, with a slight modification to overcome some of its shortcomings. Start by clipping a sling to the carabiners attached to each anchor point, just as before. Pull the section of sling between the anchor points down into a V-shape. Orient the apex of the sling in the direction of the anticipated load and tie either an overhand or a figure-of-eight on a bight into the sling. Attach a locking carabiner to the loop formed by the knot (Fig. 4-14).

By stretching the slings in the direction of the load before tying the knot, the load is distributed equally between the two anchor points. The knot then locks this configuration in place, isolating the two legs of the anchor: If the sling breaks or one of the anchor points fails, the load comes immediately and smoothly onto the remaining anchor point.

Figure 4-14. Position equalized anchor system.

The drawback of this anchor system is that the sling attached to the anchor cannot slide and distribute the load to all anchor points evenly. If the direction of loading changes even slightly, one anchor point will be loaded more than the other. This is why it's called a position equalized anchor—it's equalized in one position only. Fortunately, the direction of load rarely changes in a crevasse rescue situation, making this anchor system well suited for use on the glacier.

A two-point position equalized anchor can easily be expanded to include three or more anchor points. The more anchor points, the longer the cord needed to keep the angle between the outer strands less than 90 degrees.

Tensioned Back-up

The equalized anchor systems described above are ideal for situations in which the anchor system can be completely constructed and equalized before the load is applied. As will become clear in chapter 6, Crevasse Rescue, this is a luxury rarely encountered in a rescue situation. After a crevasse fall, the team's first priority is to transfer the weight of the climber to a solid anchor so that the team can get out of self-arrest and begin the rescue. Usually one team member places a single, quick anchor while other team members stay in self-arrest. After the weight of the climber has been transferred to this anchor, it becomes very difficult to incorporate the anchor into a self-equalized system because it is already under load.

The most practical alternative is to reinforce the first anchor with a *tensioned back-up,* a second anchor point that is attached to the load with a taut sling (Fig. 4-15). The resulting anchor system is not truly equalized because the load is not evenly shared by the anchor points. However, if the first anchor begins to slip even slightly, the tensioned back-up ensures that the second anchor will begin sharing the load immediately.

To construct a tensioned back-up, place a second anchor farther back and directly in line with the load. Clip a separate sling to the anchor holding the load, pull the sling back to a carabiner attached to the second anchor point, pull hard to apply tension, and tie the sling off.

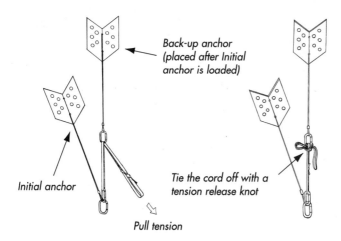

Back-up anchor
(placed after Initial
anchor is loaded)

Initial anchor

Tie the cord off with a
tension release knot

Pull tension

Figure 4-15. Tensioned back-up anchor system.

On the Ruth Glacier, Denali. Michael Strong photo

Glacier Travel Techniques

While gazing out across the broad expanse of a glacier, it's hard to imagine what could be so difficult about glacier travel. In an otherwise rugged alpine setting, the glacier can seem like a superhighway—why not just rope up and go? Although there are moments when this sense of freedom is realized, roped travel on a glacier is often a restrictive experience. The challenges imposed by maneuvering around crevasses and other obstacles and by the need to manage rope efficiently while doing so, dictate nearly every aspect of the team's movement. Progress can be maddeningly slow at times; patience can wear thin. With attention to proper technique and a little practice even a novice rope team can soon find itself moving safely and efficiently through crevassed terrain.

Although preparation is vital, the key to safe glacier travel is prevention. Being prepared for rescue is important, but it's best not to fall into a crevasse in the first place! Through thoughtful routefinding, careful rope management, and judicious use of belays, the cautious glacier traveler can avoid most crevasse hazards. This chapter examines the key principles of glacier travel in detail.

ROUTEFINDING

Routefinding is perhaps the most important safety skill in the glacier traveler's arsenal. Unfortunately, it is also one of the most difficult skills to acquire. A leader's routefinding decisions can mean the difference between an uneventful slog and an epic ordeal. A gifted routefinder is able to examine an apparently featureless glacier, predict where crevasses are most likely to be located, and choose a route that avoids most significant hazards.

Routefinding is generally the responsibility of the most experienced traveler, who takes the lead position in the rope team. The leader determines the route and sets the pace; the remaining team members take primary responsibility for rope management.

On a rope team of three, consider placing the least experienced member in the middle because at times it may be necessary to reverse directions, with the third becoming the new leader. This is not to say, however, that the middle person can be a complete beginner. Every rope team member must know how to ascend out of a crevasse, perform self-arrest, and carry out basic rescue procedures, including anchor placement. As the team moves along, trailing team members should make every effort to stay in the leader's tracks, minimizing the team's exposure to the crevasse hazard.

Although the leader is primarily responsible for routefinding decisions, it's a good idea for all team members to be alert. The best way to learn is to observe, predict, and compare your observations and predictions with those of the leader. The following suggestions are derived from many years of experience on a wide variety of glaciers. It's important, however, to remember that each glacier presents unique routefinding challenges.

- *Use vantage points to scan the glacier before stepping onto it.* A promising route that would be hard, if not impossible, to detect from the surface of the glacier may be obvious from higher up. Look for crevasse patterns, avalanche slopes, run-outs, and the location of icefalls. Early morning or evening usually provides the best light conditions for making observations; midday light tends to flatten and obscure terrain contours. Make a sketch if the routefinding is complex, marking the proposed route as well as alternate routes to use in case something doesn't work out. Maps, aerial photos, or recent snapshots can also help, especially if weather or snow conditions obscure visibility. Keep in mind that once on the glacier, access to the "big picture" is lost; things will not appear the same as when viewed from a distance.

- *Predict where crevasses are likely to occur.* When searching for crevasses from a vantage point, it's common to focus exclusively on the visible surface features. Stop and think about what's happening within the glacier as it moves along. Identify tension zones first, and use this information to predict where crevasses are most likely to be located. If possible, avoid traveling over bulges, around the outsides of bends, or along the glacier's flanks—all of these are tension zones. Scan for routes that follow concavities (compression zones) or are at least level. Again, careful study of aerial photographs can be helpful; just remember that glaciers change continually and that crevasses may or may not be visible in a photograph, depending on snowpack and lighting conditions.

- *Carefully observe the surface features when traveling.* Does the terrain match expectations from an earlier, long-distance survey? Be on constant look-out for cracks or sagging trenches in the snow surface. These usually indicate crevasses or snowbridges that have begun to deteriorate and slump under their own weight. Kneel down and look along the snow surface to better assess suspected sags. Even the slightest sags can sometimes be detected by looking for other clues, like fine windborne dust that sometimes collects in them. After a light snowfall, snow is often blown from all surfaces of the glacier except depressions.

- *Be cautious after storms have covered the glacier with a fresh blanket of snow,* especially when the glacier is not "in shape" for travel (late summer or early fall). Sagging trenches and unconsolidated snowbridges will be hard to detect. Open crevasses may be covered over. Travel in these conditions can be very dangerous. Use extreme caution!

- *Probe for crevasses.* When unsure of the stability of an area, stop and probe before proceeding. This is where a longer ice axe with a smooth shaft (as opposed to an ice tool with a padded handle) comes in handy. When a significant amount of probing is required two 3-foot sections of an avalanche probe (the kind that screw together), a portable probe, or probe ski poles are very helpful. Make sure the rope team is ready to hold a fall before probing: The rope should be taught and team members ready to self-arrest. When probing, the presence of a crevasse will be obvious, as the axe or probe will suddenly plunge through with minimal resistance. If the route must pass near the hole, enlarge it until the edges of the crevasse are found. If traversing left or right is an option, continue probing along the crevasse until it narrows and affords a safe crossing. Mark all holes well with wands.

The underlying theme of all routefinding decisions is to pay cautious, thoughtful attention to the specific details of the situation. There are no hard and fast answers when it comes to navigating over crevassed terrain; each glacier presents a unique puzzle to be solved.

ROPE MANAGEMENT

The cardinal rule of glacier travel is to keep the rope connecting team members stretched out at all times. This does not mean that the rope should be stretched so taut that it doesn't rest on the surface. Although this has been the rule in certain European traditions, it's awkward and draining to maintain and, given the shock-absorbing qualities of modern ropes, is not necessary. In most situations, it's acceptable for the rope to barely run on the snow surface without excessive tension. There are certain times, however, when the rope should be stretched very tight: when probing for a crevasse or crossing a snowbridge, for example. Serious crevasse falls have resulted from team members allowing too much slack to develop in the rope.

As the team moves, the leader sets the pace; each trailing team member is responsible for keeping the proper amount of tension in the rope ahead. Be prepared to slow down or speed up in order to keep slack from developing. For example, after topping out on a slope, a natural inclination is to speed up. Remember, however, that trailing team members are still on the slope and will probably be moving more slowly. Travel slowly until all rope members have topped out.

Rope management is relatively easy during straight-ahead travel over gentle terrain. However, when maneuvering through a crevasse field, rope management can quickly become quite challenging, requiring alertness and attention to detail.

CIRCUMVENTING CREVASSES

End Runs

The safest option for circumventing a crevasse is to pass around the end where the crevasse pinches off. Be careful on end runs because the true end of the crevasse may not be obvious. If in doubt, give the end a wide berth and probe the corner. As illustrated in Figure 5-1, circumventing a series of crevasses with end runs requires a rope team to move in a zigzag fashion.

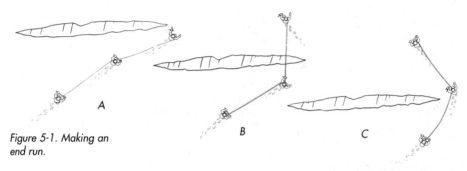

Figure 5-1. Making an end run.

When crevasses are close together and the turns are sharp, the leader will likely have to move back toward the remainder of the rope team after making the turn. To avoid excessive slack in the rope, trailing team members may have to pause, back up, or even swing wide as the leader negotiates the corner. The followers may then have to speed up, or even ask the leader to back up in order to gain enough rope to

Figure 5-2. Managing the rope to keep it perpendicular to a crevasse.

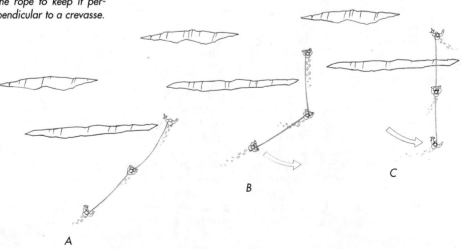

Winding through a section of the greater icefall. Muldrow Glacier, Denali.
Michael Strong photo

make the turn. Ideally, trailing team members reach the corner just as the rope is fully stretched out.

Earlier, it was mentioned that trailing team members should follow in the leader's track whenever possible to minimize the possibility of a crevasse fall. However, it may be necessary to bend this rule a little to negotiate a particularly tight matrix of crevasses. Terrain permitting, trailing team members may want to step out and "swing wide" around the ends of crevasses to keep the rope perpendicular to the crevasse, as illustrated in Figure 5-2A–C.

Traveling in Echelon

Sometimes the rope team may want to travel "in echelon". When traveling in this fashion, team members are oriented perpendicular to a series of closely spaced crevasses while moving along them, rather than being stretched out and weaving around each crevasse. As Figure 5-3 shows, should a team member take a fall while traveling in echelon, the surface members are in the best possible positions to prevent themselves from being pulled into a crevasse, for executing effective self-arrests, and placing anchors for rescue.

Figure 5-3. Traveling in echelon.

When traveling in echelon, it's extremely difficult to move along with the rope always fully stretched out between team members, since crevasse sets are not uniformly spaced, and even if they were it's unlikely that they would match a rope team's spacing pattern. As a result, traveling in echelon can be tricky, requiring great attention to rope management. While

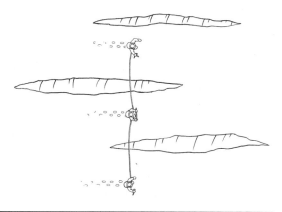

this technique should be in every glacier traveler's bag of tricks for those moments when traveling through a tight matrix of crevasses is necessary, it should be used with caution and with an understanding of its limitations.

Ultimately, the safety and efficiency of roped travel through challenging terrain depends largely on the number of rope team members and the degree to which they communicate and work together. Where a two-person team will be able to move quite efficiently through significantly broken terrain, a three-person team will move more slowly. Progress through all but the simplest crevasse fields can be a nightmare for teams of four or more.

As the complexity of rope management increases due to challenging terrain or rope team size and progress slows to a crawl, it is easy to become frustrated. Try to remain calm and patiently work through the crevasse hazard.

Practicing Rope Management

Like most skills, the key to safe and efficient rope management is practice. Don't wait until you're in the middle of a messy crevasse field to try the techniques described in this section! Rope management is easy to practice anywhere. In addition to honing individual skills, it helps build team morale and confidence. One of our favorite drills is to pick out a suitable snow field, or even a grassy lawn, and stake out some imaginary crevasses. Use pylons, ski poles, gloves, packs, or whatever is handy to mark out the ends of the crevasses, then practice moving through them as a rope team. Try different arrangements: flat terrain versus sloping, various spacing and orientation of crevasses, and different amounts of rope between climbers. Each team member should take a turn as leader, middle person, or last person; each requires slightly different skills. Trailing team members should remember to stay in the leader's tracks.

CROSSING CREVASSES

Although careful routefinding goes a long way toward avoiding crevasses, it's inevitable that sooner or later the route will be blocked by a crevasse that cannot be circumvented. When faced with this situation, the crevasse will have to be crossed on a snowbridge or jumped. The terrain will determine which option is most appropriate.

Snowbridges

Even if it were possible to meander around every crevasse with an end run, it's not an efficient way to travel. It's easy to spend as much time traveling sideways as forward over the course of the day. There comes a time when the rope team must put faith in the stability of a snowbridge. It shouldn't, however, be blind faith; it's best to first make an educated assessment of the stability of the bridge. Stability depends upon three factors: thickness of the bridge, crevasse width, and the strength of bonding between snow crystals.

- *Thickness of the bridge:* The thicker the snowbridge, the safer it is. This is one reason that glacier travel is seasonal. Generally speaking it's a good idea to avoid the accumulation zone during the fall and early winter when snow depth may still be inadequate, and in the summer when snow cover is thinning. Seasonal differences between various locations are likely to affect the decision as to where and when to travel. Research an area well while planning a trip.

- *Crevasse width:* The widest crevasses do not bridge up at all, while the narrowest ones may sport strong bridges well into the summer. The intermediate spans tend to spell trouble; bridges may form but are often very weak.

- *Strength of bonding:* The internal bonding of the snow forming the bridge is critical. The type of crystal structure in the original snowfall, wind action, and various metamorphic processes all affect the strength of the snow. During spring and early summer, snowbridges are usually rock solid after a cold, clear night (during the "freeze" portion of the melt-freeze cycle). A thin, rock hard snowbridge may be more stable than a thick snowbridge that has not undergone a melt-freeze cycle. Time of day is crucial as well; a bridge that was rock hard in the cold of early morning may be dangerously unstable later on in the day.

Because of the inherent uncertainty of assessing snowbridge strength, the team should always be prepared for the worst. Make sure that ropes between team members are fully stretched out and everyone is ready to drop into self-arrest if the bridge collapses. Place an anchor and cross the bridge on belay if the crossing is difficult, the snowbridge suspect, or the rope team is on a slope above the crevasse.

Jumping Across

Unless it's possible to get across with a short jump, try to find another way around or over the crevasse. Gauge whether the jump is level; pick another spot if the jump is uphill. Be particularly cautious if the jump is to a lower side when the downhill slope is steep. If jumping is the best option, make sure that everyone on the rope team is capable of clearing the span before the leader commits to the jump. Do not mistake the true edges of the crevasse for unstable lips of snow partially bridging a much wider span. It may be necessary to probe the leading side of the crevasse in order to identify the edge, then remove any unsupported snow and pack down a runway for a better take-off if a running start is needed.

Be prepared for a fall: Zip up your extra layers and put on a hat and gloves. Take your pack off if it's heavy (it can be pulled across on a tether). Check all rigging. And, of course,

Jumping a crevasse on the Challenger Glacier. North Cascades, Washington.
Michael Strong photo

make sure you have enough slack in the rope before jumping. The last thing you need is a pull from behind when in midair over a crevasse!

When ready, hold the axe in self-arrest position and jump. Don't be tentative or hesitant! If the jump ends up a little short of the far lip, jam your ice axe in and try to claw up and over the lip. Remember that jumping is more hazardous for the leader, who will not have the benefit of a belay from the far side of the crevasse.

Once across, the leader may want to place an anchor on the far side and belay the others across, especially if the leader's movement is restricted by nearby crevasse spans or other hazards. If the terrain affords movement, it may be best for the leader to keep the rope tight and move in synch as the second makes the jump. Terrain features will determine which decision is best. If packs are removed for jumping, they must be ferried across on a tether before the last team member crosses.

Belaying

Safe climbing is a blend of several ingredients. An experienced mountaineer who accurately evaluates hazards, makes solid routefinding decisions, and climbs with competence is less likely to fall than a novice still in the process of developing these skills. Even so, every climber falls eventually. Falling is an integral part of the climbing experience.

For back-up, climbers use rope systems, or belays, to contain and minimize the consequences of a fall. The type of belay called for depends on the situation. The team must evaluate its need for speed and/or security and then make the correct choice.

Regardless of the belay method, there are three physical components that must be integrated into all belay systems: friction, position, and anchor. If any component is missing or unsubstantial, the integrity of the belay will be compromised.

Friction is critical. Without it, even low force falls would be difficult to stop. To provide friction, pass the rope around or over a suitable object (a friction device) and allow the friction of contact to absorb the force of the fall. The object may be the torso (hip belay), a combination of the boot cuff and ice axe (boot-axe belay), or commercial belay devices designed to hold high-force falls. If you select a belay device capable of managing the force generated by the fall, the device will provide sufficient friction, so long as you hold on to the rope. When the force of the fall exceeds the device's ability to provide friction, the rope will begin to run. If this happens, you've either underestimated the forces involved or selected the wrong friction device.

Falls can happen very quickly. When providing a belay, you must be prepared to instantly hold a fall, regardless of whether you've been belaying for five minutes or two hours. Be alert at all times, learn the hand motions necessary to take rope in and feed it out and provide the braking action specific to the belay system. Friction is pointless if you don't manage the rope

Figure 5-4. The four-step sequence of hand motions. Note: The brake hand never lets go of the brake strand.

A. Start with the **brake** hand close to the belay device and the **free** hand extended.

B. Take up slack by pulling rope through the belay device with both hands. Hand positions are now reversed.

C. Extend the free hand **past** the brake hand.

D. Grab both strands with the free hand and slide the brake hand down the rope. Release the brake strand from the free hand. You're back where you started.

properly! Figure 5-4 illustrates the hand motions used to safely belay a climbing partner with a belay device.

Friction can be compromised by poor positioning. If you're not braced securely for a fall, you could be jerked off the belay stance and lose control of the rope. A belayer in *good position* is oriented in the direction of anticipated force and braced to absorb it. Whether standing upright, sitting, or hunched over in a boot-axe belay, it's vital to maintain proper body position for the belay system being used.

At some point, the force of a fall exceeds the holding threshold of even the most well-braced stance. When this happens, the team relies on an *anchor* as the primary safety backup. To protect the integrity of the anchor and maximize safety, the belayer must maintain a position in line with the anchor and anticipated direction of force, as shown in Figure 5-5.

A, Incorrect alignment

B, Correct alignment

Figure 5-5. Incorrect (A) and correct (B) belay positions while attached to an anchor

Mountaineers use a variety of belay systems to hold climbing falls. Table 5-1 provides an overview of belays relevant to glacier travel and clarifies the interaction of friction, position and anchor in each. Note that the systems are on a continuum, with the fastest, least secure systems described first, followed by ones that take longer to set up but provide more security.

Table 5-1. Belay Systems Used to Contain Low-, Moderate- and High-Force Falls.

Belay System	Friction Provided By	Belayer's Position	Type of Anchor
A. LOW FORCE			
Self-arrest—used to hold a crevasse fall or a fall by a team member on a steep slope.	The rope running over the snow and cutting into the crevasse lip. Rope stretch also absorbs force.	Stretched out with the rope taut and perpendicular to crevasses. Face down in self-arrest.	Surface team's inertia and ice axe picks digging into snow.
Self-belay—used for personal safety during a rescue.	Prusik knot gripping the rope and holding the climber.	Attached to the rope via the harness prusik or ascender.	Rope is anchored to the slope.
Prusik belay of partner—used to belay a team member out of or into a safe zone.	Prusik knot gripping the rope. Rope stretch and friction of the rope over the snow surface also absorbs force.	In a safe zone braced to absorb the force of a crevasse fall and prepared to drop into self-arrest.	Surface team's inertia and a self-arrest if needed.
B. MODERATE FORCE			
Boot-axe belay—used in firm snow to hold a moderate fall.	Rope running around a planted ice axe and over the boot cuff.	Sideways to slope in a position to effectively manage the ice axe.	Planted ice axe braced by the boot.
Harness-axe or hip-axe belay—used in firm snow to hold a moderate fall.	Rope running through a belay device or around the hip.	Standing upright on top of of the axe sling to prevent the axe from pulling out.	Planted ice axe braced by climber's weight.
Running belay—used to protect a team on an exposed slope.	Rope running through anchor points placed at intervals. Also from self-arrest.	In self-arrest or on the snow surface attempting to self-arrest.	Usually one or two well-spaced anchor points placed by the leader.
C. HIGH FORCE			
Anchored belay—belayer in the system.	Rope running through a friction device in the belayer's harness.	Attached to anchor and positioned in front of it to help dissipate force.	One or more anchor points joined into an anchor system.
Anchored belay—belayer out of the system.	Rope running through a friction device attached to the anchor.	Next to the anchor and attached to it by a tether.	One or more anchor points joined into an anchor system.

Let's examine each of the belay systems shown in Table 5-1 in more detail, beginning with the self-arrest.

Belay Systems for Low-Force Falls

The Self-Arrest

Strictly speaking, the self-arrest is not a belay at all. It's an *arrest*, a means of stopping a personal fall with the ice axe. In the context of glacier travel, however, the self-arrest is a valid belay technique, used to stop a team member from plunging into the depths of a crevasse. So long as travel is over non-technical terrain, the forces involved in a crevasse fall are usually manageable. In soft snow conditions, a self-arrest might not even be necessary; rope stretch, friction, and the rope team's inertia may dissipate so much of the force that the climbers aren't even pulled off their feet. At the other extreme, climbers may be jerked forcefully from their stances. Falls while the team is traveling on firm or icy surfaces, down a slope, or with too much slack in the rope can produce a large amount of force.

Whatever the case, team members must react reflexively to sudden, unexpected rope tension. In a severe fall, one team member will probably take the brunt of the force and be pulled down before being able to self-arrest. The climber may not have time to yell "falling!" Although the first person on a rope team is the most at risk of taking a crevasse fall, anyone can go in at any time. For these reasons, it's crucial that all team members:

- carry the ice axe using the self-arrest grip while on the glacier.
- be able to self-arrest effectively from all possible body orientations including head first and backward, with or without a pack on, and so on. Self-arrest technique, including special considerations for arresting while carrying a large pack, are addressed in appendix 2.
- stay attentive. It's easy to become bored while moving across innocuous terrain, or to drop your guard when tired. Be alert at all times and ready to self-arrest at the drop of a hat (or climber).
- keep the slack out of the rope! Many climbers have taken serious falls, subjecting themselves and team members to severe forces as a result of traveling with excessive slack in the rope. Pay attention to how lead and/or trailing team members are managing the rope.
- keep the rope perpendicular to crevasses when crossing snowbridges.

The Prusik Self-Belay

A prusik self-belay is invaluable in situations where mobility is the chief concern and when a fall will generate only a small amount of force (e.g., body weight). Climbers commonly use prusik self-belays to attach themselves indirectly to an anchor when working near a cliff edge or crevasse lip during a rescue. The prusik self-belay is simple to configure. Rig your harness prusik or ascender as illustrated in Figure 3-5.

The harness prusik can also be used to provide a belay for a rope team member, so long as the force generated by the fall is not much more than body weight.

Belaying a Teammate with the Harness Prusik

Imagine a rope team of three climbers leaving a small, wanded glacier camp. Try as they might, there will not be enough room to fully stretch out the rope between them within the confines of this small area. Unless the slack between team members is handled properly, the potential exists for a long fall should a climber go into a crevasse soon after stepping beyond the camp boundary.

The proper technique for protecting against a long fall in such situations is to "belay out" team members using the harness prusik (or ascender), as shown in Figure 5-6.

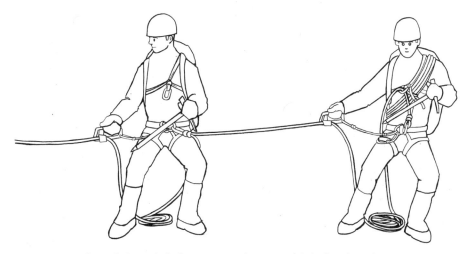

Figure 5-6. Providing a belay with the harness ascender. Note: The climbers have their axes in position to drop into self-arrest.

The second and third prepare for the leader's departure by sliding their harness prusiks along the rope toward the leader until all of the slack between each climber is taken out of the rope. When the leader starts out, the second allows the rope to slide through the harness prusik by holding open the knot (or, if a mechanical ascender is used, by depressing the cam) until the rope is fully extended (Fig. 5-7). If the leader goes into a crevasse before the rope is fully paid out, the second lets go of the prusik or ascender, allowing it to grip the rope. The second and the third should be braced for a potential fall at all times. When a fall occurs, it should not be that difficult to contain because they share the force of the fall between them. Nevertheless, they should hold their axes in the self-arrest position while belaying, just in case they get pulled off their feet. It also helps if they move to the far back of the camp before the leader starts out (staying within the safe area, of course) to avoid interfering with each other should they need to drop into self-arrest. Every bit of separation between the falling leader and other team members may count.

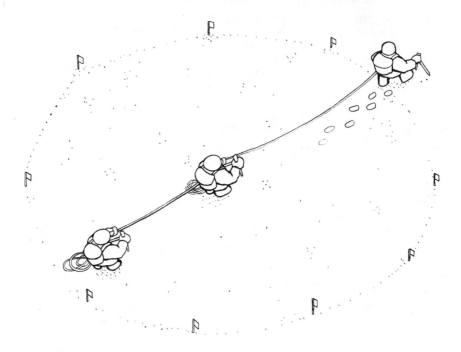

Figure 5-7. Belaying the leader with the harness prusik from a safe zone.

When the rope between the leader and the second is fully extended, the second slides the harness prusik up against the harness. This ensures that the force of a subsequent fall will come onto the rope, not the prusik. The second then follows the leader onto the glacier, now belayed by the third team member, as well as by the leader who keeps moving along. The process is repeated until the entire rope team is stretched out. As always, communication is vital in order for this to work smoothly. If a trailing team member is not prepared to move when the leading rope becomes stretched out, the trailer should call out "zero!" or "stop!" to stop progress momentarily; a call of "climbing" starts the rope team moving again.

Once the entire team is stretched out, climbers should avoid gathering together while roped up on the glacier. Breaks should be taken with the rope team fully stretched out. Stops for overnight camps on the glacier require extensive probing of a campsite, described in Camping on the Glacier.

The procedure for belaying with the harness prusik while traveling onto the glacier applies to exiting it as well. The process described above is simply reversed: The leader belays in the second, and then the first and second belay the third to safety.

Belaying with the harness prusik is simple and efficient, but is not adequate or appropriate in some situations. Do not belay with the harness prusik:

- when a fall could generate more than just a small amount of force. For example, when technical climbing is encountered right after leaving a safe zone.
- any time you could sustain an injury if pulled off your feet while belaying. For example, while belaying a climber onto the glacier from a pile of jagged rocks. In this case it's better to belay from the harness in a sitting position.
- to take excess slack out of the rope during travel. It's better to stop and back up if there's too much slack in the travel rope than it is to reel in the excess slack with the harness prusik. Never risk taking a fall on the harness prusik during travel.

Why is it acceptable to belay a partner from a safe zone with the harness prusik but unacceptable to use it to make adjustments to rope tension during travel? The main reason is that during travel, more force is exerted by a direct fall onto the harness prusik by a climber in motion. The potential for shock loading is much greater, especially if there is even the slightest amount of slack in the travel rope when a fall occurs. A climber belaying a partner onto the glacier with the harness prusik will experience far less force during a fall because the force of the fall comes onto components at the other end of the chain (the fallen climber, crevasse lip, climbing rope) and is partially dissipated by the time the belayer's harness prusik is even weighted. The belayer is also stationary, braced for the fall and better able to keep excess slack out of the rope while the climber moves away from the safe zone.

Anchored Belays—Systems for Moderate- and High-Force Falls

Although a prusik or ascender belay is an effective method for providing security when the force of a fall will be low (e.g., a short crevasse fall on a taut rope), a more sturdy *anchored belay* must be provided when the potential exists for moderate or serious falls. Provide an anchored belay for a climber who:

- is on steep and exposed terrain, such as above a cliff or crevasse;
- is attempting a wide crevasse crossing on a fragile snow-bridge;
- must climb down one wall of a crevasse and then up the other wall; or
- must cross a tenuous snowbridge when the rope runs more or less parallel to the crevasse.

Providing a boot-axe belay. Mount Baker, Washington. Michael Strong photo

There are several options for providing an anchored belay. The *boot-axe, harness-axe,* and *running* belays are good choices for protecting *moderate* falls. When the potential exists for a *high-force* fall, place an anchor system (constructed from conventional ice or snow anchors), attach to it, and belay from the harness or directly from the anchor.

The Boot-Axe Belay

When a belay is needed in a hurry, nothing is faster than a boot-axe belay. However, *it cannot be called on to hold a significant amount of force!* In ideal snow conditions (firm snow) it can hold a short, moderate fall. A more forceful fall will cause the rope to run around the boot or rip the axe out.

The boot-axe belay has other limitations. It's awkward to execute on a level surface. The most stable position is achieved when one foot is placed well above the other, as shown in Figure 5-8. The belaying motions are also awkward. During a fall it's usually necessary to remove the free hand from the rope and jam it down onto the head of the ice axe for added security.

The boot-axe belay is executed as follows:

- *Assess the snow conditions:* The boot-axe belay requires firm snow. If the snow is unconsolidated, use another belay method. Loose, cold snow simply can not be packed into an adequate platform and will not hold the axe. Wetter, warmer snow can be packed down to form a platform large enough for the uphill boot and ice axe.
- *Plant the axe:* Angle the ice axe slightly uphill and plunge it in as far as it will go, with the pick pointing across the

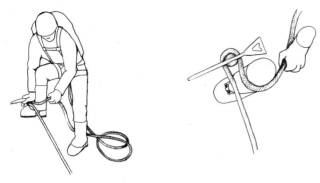

Figure 5-8. The boot-axe belay.

slope and away from you. Ideally, the shaft will be completely buried in the snow, with only the head protruding.

- *Get in position to belay:* Face sideways in the direction the pick is pointing and place the uphill foot firmly against the downhill side of the ice axe. Plant the downhill foot securely somewhat lower, keeping the leg as straight as possible. It's important to be comfortably in balance.
- *Configure the rope:* Configure the rope such that it comes over the boot, around the ice axe, and back around the boot cuff, as shown in Figure 5-8.

During a fall, friction is provided by wrapping the rope around the boot cuff with the brake hand. The free hand presses down on the head of the ice axe. When the climber moves on, the free hand assists in taking up or letting out rope.

The Harness-Axe Belay

The harness-axe belay is similar to the boot-axe belay in its reliance on the planted ice axe as a makeshift belay anchor. Its main advantage is comfort and ease of rope management. Rather than hunching over to belay at ground level, the belayer stands upright and belays from the harness, making for better security, balance, and comfort (Fig. 5-9).

This method provides more holding power than the boot-axe belay because the force of a fall pulls the climber downward, more firmly into the belay stance. Furthermore, there's no chance that the planted axe will be levered downhill as in the boot-axe belay, because the belayer stands on the sling in front of the axe placement. The additional friction in the system at the ice axe carabiner and the belay device is helpful as well.

Set up the belay as follows:

- *Assess the snow conditions:* Firm snow is required for this belay, as explained for the boot-axe belay.
- *Attach a carabiner to a loop on the axe:* Girth-hitch a small sling onto the shaft of the ice axe, slide it up as far as it

Figure 5-9. The harness-axe belay.

will go and clip a carabiner to it. If a long sling is used for an ice axe tether, clip a carabiner to the wrist loop after shortening the tether by wrapping it around the shaft and over the head of the axe several times. The final length of the sling should place the carabiner within three or four inches of the axe shaft.

• *Plant the axe:* Angle the ice axe slightly uphill and plunge it into the snow as far as possible. Again, the more axe you can bury in the snow, the stronger the belay. The loop with the attached carabiner should rest on the snow surface near the head of the axe.

• *Get into position:* Face sideways with the uphill foot on the sling directly next to the axe. The sling should be long enough to leave the carabiner exposed just downhill of your boot. Plant the downhill foot securely, placing yourself in a balanced position.

• *Set up the belay:* Clip the rope from the climber through the carabiner on the snow surface and then into a belay device in the seat harness. The uphill hand should act as the brake hand. Take up slack, and hold a fall with standard belaying motions.

Lacking a belay device, it's easy to modify this system to incorporate a body belay; simply wrap the rope around your hips instead of using a belay device. Be sure to add a guide carabiner at the front of the harness to prevent the rope from sliding off the hips during a fall, as illustrated in Figure 5-10. The guide carabiner must not slide around the side of the harness under force; attach it so that it stays put.

The Running Belay

The running belay is a technique that allows a team to move relatively quickly without compromising safety. It's commonly used in situations where a self-arrest would be inadequate to hold the force of a fall, such as when traversing an ice slope or climbing terrain too steep for an arrest to be effective. During a running belay, the leader places anchor points at fixed intervals, clipping the rope through them before continuing on. Following team members clip past the anchors as they reach them. If the running belay is for a single pass along the slope, the end removes the anchors. Before running out of protection, the leader stops, builds a stationary anchor, and then belays fellow climbers in. At this point the leader can collect anchors (from the end) and resume climbing, or the end can set out on lead.

In a running belay, the number of anchors you'll need depends on the security of the placements and the climbing difficulty. If the climbing is easy and the placements solid, one anchor point may be enough to hold a fall. As difficulty increases and/or the quality of anchor

Figure 5-10. Hip-axe belay with a guide carabiner.

placements decreases, several anchor points stretched along
the length of the rope may be required to share the load and
reduce the length of a potential fall.

Figure 5-11. The
running belay.

Figure 5-11 shows a team of three protected by a single
anchor point. In this situation the leader should attach two
carabiners to the anchor slings. This arrangement allows the
middle to clip into the trailing rope before detaching from the
carabiner on the lead rope. At no point will the team be
detached from the anchor if the middle follows this sequence.
When the team is protected by just a single anchor, the end
must not remove it until the leader has placed the next anchor
along the route.

Belaying from an Anchor System

There are some situations in which the belays described
above are simply not adequate. When a leader is crossing a
wide crevasse on a questionable snowbridge or on a steep
downslope, or when snow conditions are not suitable for an
axe or running belay, it's best to set up an anchored belay that
is more secure. If there's any danger of such a severe, high-
force fall, take the time to place an anchor system. Select suitable anchors (as previously discussed in chapter 4) for the
snow conditions and place them to hold in the direction of
anticipated force.

Option 1: Belaying in the system—Sit on a pack or Ensolite
pad, and either tie into the anchor using the climbing rope, or

clip into it with a daisy chain or sling girth-hitched to the front of the harness. Sit in line with the anticipated direction of force and snug against the anchor. Belay from a belay device or Müenter hitch on the seat harness (Fig. 5-12).

Option 2: Belaying out of the system—Another option is to attach to the anchor and belay directly from it with a belay device or Müenter hitch (Fig. 5-13). If the climber falls and requires a rescue, it's not necessary to perform a belay escape as would be required when belaying from the harness. When belaying out of the system (i.e., directly off of the anchor), the climber can be quickly tied off as the first step in the rescue process. While this option is not as important to a three-person rope team, it saves valuable time and energy for the lone rescuer of a two-person team.

Figure 5-12. Belaying in the system. Note: The climber attaches to the anchor and belays from the harness.

Because there is no belayer in the system to mediate the force of a fall, the anchor system must be absolutely bombproof when belaying directly from the anchor. For this reason, belaying from the harness is preferable in most cases.

Figure 5-13. Belaying out of the system. Note: The climber attaches to the anchor and belays directly from it.

TRAVEL DURING INCLEMENT WEATHER

Snow storms, dense clouds, blowing snow, and other low-visibility conditions are not uncommon in the mountains, and can make any mountaineering expedition more challenging. Inclement weather is particularly dangerous for the glacier traveler. On the relatively flat terrain of a glacier it's easy to become disoriented and drift off course. Routefinding also becomes impossible as visibility drops; the routefinder can no longer locate tension zones and analyze terrain to avoid crevasse fields, and local clues like sags and bumps become much harder to discern. The chances of suffering a crevasse fall increase greatly. In short, glacier travel during inclement conditions should be attempted in only the most desperate circumstances. The wise traveler will stay in camp and wait for better weather.

Because mountain weather can change rapidly, it's likely that any team spending a significant amount of time in the mountains will be caught out in a storm sooner or later. Everyone must be prepared with the essentials: proper clothing, shelter, food and water, map and compass (and the knowledge of how to use them), crevasse rescue gear, and sufficient wands to mark the route. An altimeter is also a useful routefinding aid.

The most effective insurance against becoming lost or drifting off course while traveling in poor visibility is a line of wands that marks the route. Use wands to identify a return route in bad weather and to mark hazards such as crevasses. With the route wanded, travel is safer and more efficient during a storm, or even at night if the weather is decent.

When conditions begin deteriorating, place wands along the route, spaced no farther apart than the distance from the first person in the climbing party to the last one, with the rope(s) fully stretched out. Following this strategy, a party of six traveling in two-rope teams of three will place about 18 wands for every mile of glacier travel, as opposed to the independent three-person rope team, who will need to place twice as many wands. Resist the temptation to place wands farther apart; in extremely foul weather visibility may be reduced to mere feet. In such conditions, the climbing party's only hope of a safe return will be to travel from wand to wand.

The leader usually carries a quiver of wands and places them on the original pass over the route. When the last person on the rope (or in the climbing party) reaches the last-placed wand and yells "wand," the leader places another one. On the return (final) pass over the route the last person in the climbing party waits at the end wand until the leader locates the next one along the route. With that wand located, the last person stows the wand and the party moves on, traveling wand to wand.

Establish a consistent "marking code" when placing wands. For example, two wands placed in an X usually indicate a crevasse; two wands together pointing the same way indicate the new direction of travel at a corner; and wands that are angled slightly (like a pointer) identify the direction of travel. Whatever marking code is used, be sure that all team members understand it thoroughly.

Wands are available commercially or can be homemade from tomato stakes. Some climbers prefer wire wands used for marking construction projects because they are more compact, as light or lighter than an equivalent number of stakes and they come with large, highly visible flags.

Making Wands

To make wands, purchase a suitable quantity of tomato stakes 3 to 4 feet long—long enough to be clearly seen while remaining upright in loose snow. Wands longer than about 4 feet are awkward to carry. The best material for the flags is either 2-inch-wide fluorescent tape or flagging. When using adhesive tape, simply fold a strip of tape over onto itself around the top of the stake. Fluorescent flagging works very well too, but it's not adhesive, making it harder to secure to the stake. With flagging, cut a 2- to 3-inch slot in the top of the stake, insert a strip into the slot, and tie the flagging off. Finish by taping the top of the stake closed. It can be difficult to find flagging or tape wider than 2 inches, but it can be special ordered by most retailers. Just be sure to order a durable product. Some kinds of flagging become brittle and break apart in high winds, leaving an almost invisible wand to look for.

TRAVELING ON SKIS OR SNOWSHOES

There are times when it's necessary to use skis or snowshoes to travel efficiently. If flotation is the main concern, either works well. Snowshoe travel is somewhat slower and more cumbersome, but allows better control on downhills and during tight maneuvering, especially when pulling a sled.

Skiing is slightly faster but requires more skill. Skiing in synchrony down steeper slopes on the glacier can be very dangerous unless performed by a well-practiced and experienced rope team. The team must remain perpendicular to crevasses and manage the rope properly while controlling its speed. When a team member crosses a snowbridge on skis, the other team members should brace with skis perpendicular to a snowbridge and sidestep along, maintaining rope tension and holding poles in the self-arrest position in preparation for a fall. If a team member goes into a crevasse, an immediate, controlled self-arrest by other team members is not always possible, subjecting the fallen climber to a more severe fall. It's a good idea to place the most skilled skier at the back of the team to maximize the chances of an effective team arrest.

A more conservative technique is for the team to carefully snowplow on downslopes to maintain control and prevent slack from developing. Consider having less-skilled skiers use skins for descending steep downhills. If skins aren't available, skis can be converted to "skinny snowshoes" by throwing a dozen or more half hitches of cord along the length of the ski to effectively prevent the ski from sliding. Metal-edged skis require duct-taping to avoid cutting the cord.

When skiing on a glacier, every team member should be equipped with ski poles that have self-arrest grips. Skis must be equipped with safety straps; the spring-loaded ski brakes used by most alpine skiers are unsuitable for glacier travel. After a fall, the fallen skier can remove the skis, letting them hang by the straps while ascending out of the crevasse.

Do not travel unroped, even when using skis or snowshoes. Although skis and snowshoes distribute a traveler's weight over a larger surface area, a crevasse fall is still possible. In addition, crevasses are generally harder to detect in the snowy conditions that necessitate the use of skis or snowshoes.

Avoid stepping on the rope with metal-edged skis or the sharp binding claws of the snowshoe. To keep a lead rope from under foot when moving along, take a small bight of rope in one hand and give it a small flip as your hand moves forward with each step. With a little fiddling, it's possible to find an arrangement that stays on a ski pole.

Finally, consider traveling with the foot ascender already attached to your boot when snowshoeing (and when skiing if the rigging system allows unhindered travel). After a fall it may be difficult to reach down, take the snowshoe off, and put the foot prusik on. There's also the risk of dropping the snowshoe into the crevasse. It's possible to ascend the rope with snowshoes on if the crevasse is wide enough.

Camping on the Muldrow Glacier, Denali. Michael Strong photo

Camping on a glacier is a unique and wonderful experience. While wrapped in the warmth of a sleeping bag, the occasional groans and pops of the ice provide a reminder that sleep will come while relaxing on a river of moving ice. Contrary to popular myth, camping on a glacier is not particularly dangerous and, in fact, can be much safer than other places in the mountains.

The key to safe camping is to choose a proper campsite. Pick a spot far enough away from surrounding heights to be safe from icefall, rockfall, and avalanches. Remember that these hazards can travel a great distance onto the glacier from the base of the wall.

If possible, camp in a compression zone where crevasses have been squeezed together. Once a safe location is chosen, probe for crevasses. This can be a time-consuming task, as the entire circumference of the potential camp must be probed, with the distance between probes no greater than about 18 inches apart. Use the full length of a 12-foot avalanche probe. If a crevasse is found, move to a different location. Once the outer perimeter is probed, probe through the middle of the camping area in an X pattern. Keep the prober(s) on belay until it feels safe to gather together in the campsite and unrope. Wand the outer perimeter immediately, taking care to place the wands no farther out than the probed area. Do not leave the confines of the wanded campsite without being roped up and on belay.

A difficult issue for glacier campers is the disposal of solid waste. The best choice is to leave the glacier and take care of business in a location where contamination of the water supply is least likely: on a rocky moraine, or better yet, in some soil. If the soil is too thin to dig a cathole for waste disposal, and the location is remote, use the smear technique. Smear the feces into as thin a layer as possible on a flat surface, preferably a rock. In sunny weather, the combined actions of the sun and wind will dry out, disintegrate, and disperse this thin layer of feces over a relatively short period of time.

If it's not possible to retreat to an unvisited moraine (e.g., while camping on a large remote glacier), solid waste must be disposed of in some other way. For many years the standard practice has been to defecate on the glacial surface and toss the solid waste into a crevasse with a shovel. This is still an acceptable option in remote areas. For larger groups or more permanent camps, it may be more efficient to use doubled plastic garbage bags (biodegradable are best) held open by wands or some other means. Before they get too full, toss the bags into the deepest available crevasse.

Although tossing solid waste into crevasses may be the only viable option on excursions to remote areas, it is not acceptable on more popular routes. On these routes, the accumulated waste has already begun to create a health hazard. The belief that feces will be "ground up" and somehow cleansed by the milling action of the glacier before it reaches lower elevation is, for the most part, wishful thinking. In actuality, fecal decay is prolonged by cold temperatures, and harmful pathogens such as *Giardia lamblia* are capable of surviving in the cold. On cold, remote glaciers, climbers are simply putting solid waste into temporary frozen storage, with the polluting effects of this practice delayed for many years.

Not so for smaller glaciers with summer runoff. During summer, fecal matter is washed out of the glacier by meltwater, polluting the entire watershed. The days of being able to drink straight from streams draining the glaciers of temperate regions are long past. In popular areas, management agencies have taken action. On Mount Rainier, for example, climbers are required to use portable toilets installed by the National Park Service or to carry solid waste out in either a double-bag system or a "poop tube."

The *blue-bag* system was initiated by the park service on popular glacier routes, and gets its name from the color of the inner bag in this two-bag design. Place the hand inside the blue bag, gather up the waste with the enveloped hand, turn the bag inside-out, and then seal the bag securely. Place the blue bag inside the outer plastic bag and tie the outer bag securely. Once out of the mountains, deposit the waste at an appropriate disposal facility. Do not drop the bags down a toilet hole.

The *poop tube* is simply a plastic tube containing some kitty litter (for absorbency and odor control) with a tight-fitting screw cap on one end. It was developed in Yosemite for use by big wall climbers as an alternative to tossing solid waste off of climbs, the accepted protocol many years ago. Defecate into a paper bag, wrap the bag up and place it into the tube. Once out of the mountains, the contents of the tube (litter, paper bag, and solid waste) can be deposited in an outhouse, a definite advantage over the blue-bag system. You can make your own tube by cutting an appropriate length of 4-inch PVC pipe, gluing a solid cap onto one end, and a screw-cap fitting on the other.

Two other commonsense rules for overnight stays are worth mentioning. First, when in a popular area, make an effort to camp away from the primary travel route. This reduces impact and makes the experience better for everyone. Second, scour the campsite carefully when breaking camp. Pick up any scraps of food and trash, and don't leave any wands behind.

Each climber is ethically responsible for knowing and applying zero-impact travel and camping techniques, and legally responsible for knowing and following management agency regulations for the area. Too often, mountaineers have caused excessive impacts, placing recreational interests and goals above the interests of environmental preservation. These zones, especially the few areas of vegetation, are extremely fragile. The increasing popularity of glacier travel means that each individual must make an extra effort to help keep impacts to a minimum.

Practicing self-rescue, Mount Baker, Washington. Tony Jewell photo

Crevasse Rescue

Of all the hazardous situations that a climber faces, few can compare with an unexpected crevasse fall. The sheer suddenness of the event can be quite disorienting, for the climber as well as the team members remaining on the surface. One moment you're strolling casually across a seemingly innocuous expanse of snow, the next you're scrambling to rescue a fallen team member from the depths of the glacier. The time has come for the team to find out how well honed their rescue skills are.

There are two keys to proficient crevasse rescue: proper preparation, the components of which have been addressed in previous chapters, and efficient execution. A skilled rescuer can:

- identify the most appropriate rescue system to employ based on the particulars of the situation;
- implement each step in the rescue process calmly and efficiently even in the most demanding circumstances; and
- improvise safe and effective alternative rescue systems when required (e.g., when conventional gear fails or is missing, or when unusual conditions render standard systems unsafe or ineffective).

Knowledge alone is not enough. Expertise is developed from many hours spent practicing the rescue skills and then applying them in simulations and real rescue situations.

So where does the novice start? It's critical to first develop a conceptual understanding of the rescue sequence, for several reasons. First, the core elements of this sequence are consistent across most rescue situations, providing a degree of consistency from one circumstance to another. Second, even a relatively inexperienced team member can be a valuable asset during a rescue when equipped with a mental map of the rescue sequence. In practice, implementing a rescue system involves many steps that build on each other, and if all team members know what needs to be done next, no matter what their place in the rope team, the fallen climber will be rescued.

Figure 6-1 provides a broad overview of the steps in the rescue process. A key feature illustrated by this overview is the continual, active engagement of *both* the surface team and the climber in the rescue process: The surface team doesn't assume that the fallen climber will ascend out of the crevasse; likewise, the fallen climber does not simply wait for a rescue from above. It's a team effort from start to finish. This unified effort is the key to efficiency. Lacking a common understanding of the sequence of events, the team may sputter along wasting valuable time and effort, and perhaps even compromising the safety of the operation.

Crevasse Fall

Surface Team | Fallen Climber

Surface Team

1. Arrest and hold the fall.

2. Place an anchor.

3. Transfer the load to the anchor and tie the rope off.

4. Reinforce the anchor.

5. Check on the fallen climber and pad the crevasse lip for rescue.

6. Select and implement the rescue option.

7. Tend to the climber

Fallen Climber

1. Warn team members by yelling "falling."

2. Recover from the fall and prepare to ascend the rope.

3. Ascend to the crevasse lip.

4. Exit over the crevasse lip.

5. Tend to physical needs.

Figure 6-1. The sequence of events following a crevasse fall.

The following section provides an overview of the rescue process from both perspectives, beginning with efforts of the climber in the crevasse.

A. SELF-RESCUE—AN OVERVIEW

The Self-Rescue Sequence for a Fallen Climber

While the decisions facing a fallen climber are less complex than those confronting the surface team, they are just as crucial to the outcome of the rescue. If uninjured, the climber must work methodically through the following rescue steps:

• Step 1—*Warn team members by yelling "falling."*

A falling climber can exert considerable force on the remaining team members, dragging them along the surface or pulling them off a precarious stance (e.g., on a downhill slope). For this reason, it's crucial to warn others at the first hint of a possible crevasse fall. Of course, this will lead to false alarms as you punch through crusts, encounter natural hollows, and so on. Do not be embarrassed. Those extra milliseconds of warning are critical to allow team members to brace for the fall.

• Step 2—*Recover from the fall and prepare to ascend the rope.*

After the fall, your first priority is self-preservation. After a quick check for injuries, put on an extra layer, with emphasis on handwear. A sip of water and a quick bite can do wonders for calming the nerves and focusing your mind on the tasks at hand.

Ascending the rope is not the only possible exit strategy. Take stock of all the options. Is there a snow ramp within easy reach that you can be lowered to and then climb up? Rule out the easy exits before you commit to ascending the rope.

If there's no easy way out, prepare to ascend by sliding your harness prusik up the rope and slipping your foot prusik on. Unclip from the chest harness, because it's not needed to maintain an upright position unless you're carrying a heavy (backpacking weight) pack or pulling a sled. Self rescue for a climber wearing a heavy pack or pulling a sled is described in later sections.

• Step 3—*Ascend to the crevasse lip.*

Alternate between sitting in the seat harness and standing in the foot loop(s). The action is reminiscent of an inchworm moving up a vine. Totally unweight the foot prusik and loosen the knot before attempting to slide the prusik up the rope, since the smallest amount of weight on the knot will make the cord difficult to move. It's not necessary to wait for the rescuers to reinforce the anchor before ascending. Chances are that at least one anchor point will be firmly in place by the time you're ready to begin. If not, the small movements involved in ascending will not significantly alter the load on the surface rescuers. Figures 6-2 and 6-3 illustrate two different ascending techniques.

Slide the foot prusik up while sitting on the seat harness prusik.

Transfer the weight to the foot prusik.

Move the seat harness prusik up while standing in the foot prusik.

Figure 6-2. Self-rescue using a harness and foot prusik.

Slide the foot prusik up while sitting on the seat harness prusik.

Stand up in your prusik slings. Slide the unweighted harness ascender up the rope.

Sit back on the harness ascender. Repeat the sequence.

Figure 6-3. The Texas prusik system using mechanical ascenders.

- Step 4—*Exit over the crevasse lip.*

Ideally, you'll reach the lip of the crevasse at about the same time that a surface rescuer reaches the edge to check on you. Getting over the crevasse lip can be very difficult, even if the lip has been padded by rescuers on the surface. A helping hand from above can save a lot of time and effort. If the rope has cut well into the lip, a blocking overhang may prevent you from reaching up to the rescuer. When this happens, another form of assistance will be required from above. A set of aiders (improvised from webbing) fixed to the rope with a prusik knot and lowered over the edge can serve as "stairs" you can climb up.

- Step 5—*Tend to physical needs.*

A climber who's been able to ascend the rope will most likely be uninjured. Nevertheless, it's a good idea to check for minor injuries. Keep in mind that you may have expended a fair amount of energy getting out of the crevasse. Eat some food and drink some water before continuing on your way.

Practicing Fixed-Rope Ascension

Efficiently ascending a vertical rope is much more diffi-cult than it appears, particularly if there isn't a wall to sta-bilize against during the ascent. Practice this skill at home first. Find any suitable high anchor: a barn with sturdy rafters, a tall playground structure, or a tree with high stur-dy branches. Create the anchor by slinging the branch or cross-rail you have chosen with webbing and carabiners (incorporating redundancy as usual). Then configure the rope as shown in Figure 6-4. Note that a single rope is all that's needed, even with a belay option built in!

Ascend up the single strand of rope. Reverse the process and move back down the rope. Rig a heavy pack and work through the process of removing it if you plan on traveling on a glacier while wearing a heavy pack.

Figure 6-4. Ascending a fixed rope with a belay option.

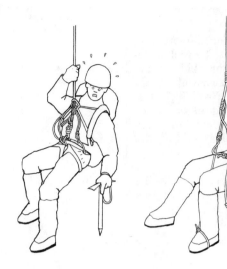

| After the fall, the chest harness prevents you from being pulled backward. Prepare to ascend the rope. Keep your pack on for now. | Next, ascend just far enough to unweight the climbing rope. Slide the pack prusik up as high as it will go, detach from the rope, and let the pack hang by its prusik attachment to the rope. | Ascend the rope, free of the pack's weight. |

Figure 6-5. Self-rescue—managing a pack rigged with a pack prusik.

Self-Rescue with a Heavy Pack

As discussed in chapter 3 it's necessary to modify the basic rigging system when carrying a heavy pack. You must be able to take your pack off without dropping it into the crevasse, ascend the rope to safety, and then retrieve the pack once on the surface. Several ways to rig for travel when carrying a heavy pack are described and illustrated in chapter 3. The merits and limitations of each method are also discussed. Review this information (if necessary) before reading on. Once you've selected a rigging option, practice the ascending sequence prior to traveling on the glacier. The ascending sequence for each of the rigging options is shown in Figures 6-5 and 6-6.

Ascending Past a Sled

After a fall with a sled, you must be able to ascend free of the sled, as it's virtually impossible to drag the sled up the rope with you. Because the sled is attached to the rope, it will be hanging above you after a fall. For this reason, you must first detach from the rope, then ascend past the sled to the surface, as shown in Figure 6-7. As when carrying a heavy pack, it's best to clip into the rope, rather than tying in.

Figure 6-6. Self-rescue—managing packs clipped to the climbing rope.

The self-rescue sequence when the pack is attached via a tether to the clip-in loop goes as follows:

1. Ascend the rope with the pack still on. After a couple of ascending sequences, slack develops in the rope's attachment to the seat harness carabiner.

2. With the pack still on, unclip the rope from the seat harness carabiner. It's necessary to keep the pack on because the pack is attached to the loop you're trying to detach from the seat harness carabiner. If you take the pack off first, the clip-in loop is weighted, making the process of unclipping from the rope much more difficult.

3. Once you've unclipped yourself from the rope, take the pack off, leaving it dangle from the harness clip-in loop, as shown above.

4. Continue ascending under body weight.

5. When rigged as shown, the harness tether on the foot prusik serves as a back-up for the seat harness prusik.

When the pack is clipped to the rope, you will have to ascend with half the pack's weight, a challenging undertaking with a heavy pack. Other drawbacks include the following:

1. You cannot readily access any pack compartments if the pack is hanging below you on the rope.

2. The pack may catch on the lip of the crevasse, making exit from the crevasse somewhat cumbersome.

This method of tethering the pack is better suited for use with lighter summit packs.

Passing the sled's attachment(s) to the rope will require you to remove—one at a time—the harness and foot prusiks upon reaching the sled's attachment(s) to the rope, then re-attach them once above these points. This task is relatively easy when using mechanical ascenders, which can be unclipped and reclipped around the sled's attachment(s) to the rope.

This process is more time consuming when using prusiks, as you'll have to remove the harness prusik from the rope. When the harness prusik is removed, you'll be attached to the rope with only the foot prusik. For safety and simplicity, it is best to use a foot prusik with a built-in harness tether as illustrated in chapter 3.

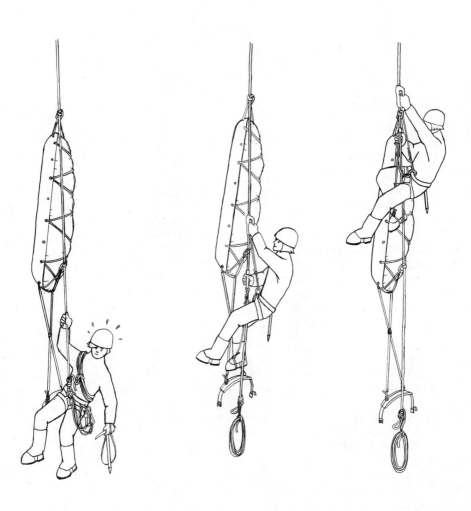

Figure 6-7. Ascending past a sled.

A crevasse fall can be very confusing for an unprepared surface team. What should be done first? Put in an anchor? Check on the fallen climber? Wait and see if the climber can ascend out of the crevasse? As mentioned earlier, it's vital that the surface team have a well-structured plan that is known to and has been practiced by all team members. The seven-step sequence for a surface rescue team (listed in Figure 6-1) is described in detail below.

• Step 1—*Arrest and hold the fall.*

As explained in chapter 5, the self-arrest is the primary belay system for the rope team on a glacier. When a teammate goes into a crevasse, it's imperative that surface members react with lightning quick self-arrests.

• Step 2—*Place an anchor.*

After the fall has been contained, one of the rescuers must release from self-arrest and place a solid anchor. But which one? Terrain features, differences in ability, weight, strength, distribution of anchor materials, and possible injury to a rescuer may all play a role in this decision. Regardless of choice, it is imperative that the rescuers communicate with each other and understand the implications of their decision in shaping the remainder of the rescue.

The main advantages of having the middle person place the anchor from a fully stretched out rope configuration are:

a) if something goes wrong, the end person has more room in which to self-arrest and bring the rope team to a stop;

b) it takes less time to place the anchor, as neither climber has to move from his/her respective locations;

c) there is little risk of either climber taking a crevasse fall because he/she stays in place until the anchor is placed and the load transferred to it (provided, of course, that neither rescuer is perched on a snowbridge).

The main advantages of having the end person swing past the middle to place an anchor closer to the crevasse are:

a) the middle person is probably already holding the bulk of the climber's weight while in self-arrest, so there's no need to transfer this load to the end person (as there would be if the middle person were to place the anchor);

b) the amount of surface rope available for rescue is maximized because the anchor is placed closer to the crevasse. As a result, the rescuers have more rescue options available to them. For this reason alone, it's considered standard protocol to have the end person place the anchor between the middle person and the crevasse. Figure 6-8 shows the end person swinging past the middle to place an anchor closer to the crevasse lip.

In review, if conditions are optimal for very secure self-arrests (i.e., low angle, firm snow), it's preferable to maximize rescue rope by having the end person swing past the middle

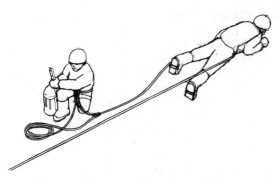

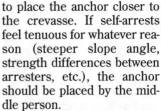

to place the anchor closer to the crevasse. If self-arrests feel tenuous for whatever reason (steeper slope angle, strength differences between arresters, etc.), the anchor should be placed by the middle person.

Figure 6-8. Swinging past the middle person to place an anchor.

In most situations one well-placed anchor will hold the weight of a fallen climber. In less than ideal conditions, however, more than one anchor may have to be placed before the self-arrest can be released. In particularly unstable conditions three pieces may have to be placed. If only one anchor is available, the rescuer placing the anchor may have to bury a pack, snowshoes, or other items in order to construct a solid anchor system. The rescuer may also choose to self-belay to the other surface team member (who's in self-arrest) to retrieve additional protection points.

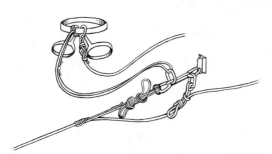

Immediately after placing the anchor, the rescuer attaches directly to it on a sling (or daisy chain) girth-hitched to the seat harness (Fig. 6-9).

Note: As an alternative (e.g. a long sling is not available), the rescuer can clip a section of the climbing rope to the anchor for safety, as shown in Figure 6-10.

Figure 6-9. Attaching to the anchor with a sling.

• Step 3—*Transfer the load to the anchor and tie the rope off.*

The rescuer at the anchor ties a prusik (or a Klemheist) knot onto the loaded rope with a cordelette, and ties the cordelette off to the anchor with a tension release knot. With the tension release mechanism in place, the self-arrest can be released and the climber's weight slowly transferred to the anchor. The self-arrester must be ready to fall back into self-arrest should the anchor move or appear tenuous.

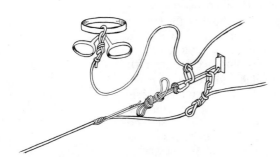

As soon as the self-arrest is released, the rescuer at the anchor backs up the tension-release mechanism by tying the (now slack) climbing rope directly to the anchor with a backed-up Müenter hitch on a separate locking carabiner. Separate carabiners facilitate easy management of the tie-off knots should the fallen climber have to be lowered later.

Figure 6-10. Attaching to the Anchor with a Section of the Climbing Rope.

Tension-Release Knots—Essential Components of Rescue Systems

A tension-release knot (Fig. 6-11 & 6-12) is any knot that can be untied and released in a controlled manner while under tension. The Müenter hitch is the best choice because it can be tied quickly, is easy to manage under load, and holds effectively when tied with a single strand of cord or webbing. The mariner's knot also works, but only when tied with a double strand of cord. Once the tension-release mechanism holds the load, the rope is tied off to the anchor with a backed-up Müenter hitch.

Why is it important to incorporate tension-release knots into the rescue system? Why not simply clip the cordelette or sling into the anchor and, subsequently, tie off the rope with a figure -of-eight on a bight or a clove hitch? The main reason is that the system has a lowering option built into it. It may turn out that the best choice is to lower the fallen climber to a snowbridge, ramp, or constriction for an easy walk out or short climb. The climber may also have to be lowered after being inadvertently hauled up against the crevasse roof or lip later in the rescue. If the cordelette or sling is tied off to the anchor with a tension-release knot, the load can be readily transferred onto the climbing rope. And if the rope is tied off with a Müenter hitch, the climber can be quickly lowered in a controlled fashion.

In general, rescue protocol dictates that a lowering option be built into any raising system. The rescuers may find out that it's necessary to place another anchor system in order to free up more rope for rescue, or to transfer the rescue to another rope (e.g., when a blocking overhang prevents rescue). In either case, the load will have to be transferred from the initial system to an alternate one. A tension-release mechanism built into the anchor tie-off facilitates the process of modifying the initial rescue set-up. A rescue team must not limit its options, as the course of events in any rescue is unpredictable.

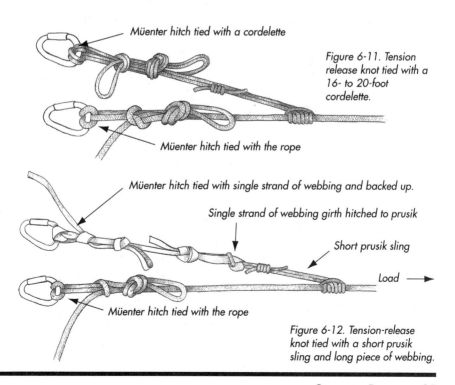

Müenter hitch tied with a cordelette

Müenter hitch tied with the rope

Figure 6-11. Tension release knot tied with a 16- to 20-foot cordelette.

Müenter hitch tied with single strand of webbing and backed up.

Single strand of webbing girth hitched to prusik

Short prusik sling

Load →

Müenter hitch tied with the rope

Figure 6-12. Tension-release knot tied with a short prusik sling and long piece of webbing.

- Step 4—*Reinforce the anchor.*

Although a single, solid anchor is usually adequate to hold a fallen climber, an anchor system consisting of at least two anchor points is necessary to accommodate the greater forces generated during a raising rescue. A *tensioned back-up* is the best choice for joining the two pieces because one anchor point will probably be holding the load at this point in the rescue process.

Note: Building safe and efficient anchor systems requires practice. Failure of an anchor could be fatal to the entire team. Be sure you have a rock-solid understanding of the anchor systems described in chapter 4, and have practiced building them in simulated rescue scenarios. An actual crevasse rescue situation is no place to be practicing your skills.

- Step 5—*Check on the fallen climber and pad the crevasse lip for rescue.*

Contact with the fallen climber must be made as soon as possible. After all, the climber's condition remains a mystery until verbal or visual contact has been made. Is the climber ascending the rope to safety? Is he/she unconscious and in need of urgent assistance? The rescuers must work quickly, aware that their teammate's well-being may depend upon their performance.

Never compromise your personal safety for the sake of speed. The rescuer who released from self-arrest should not approach the lip until the anchor has been reinforced. The last thing you need is two climbers loading a single anchor point.

While waiting for the anchor to be reinforced, the middle person unclips from the rope, unties the clip-in knot, and slides the harness prusik along the rope toward the anchor (i.e., into position for a secure self- belay). By untying the knot in the middle of the rope:

a) a long strand of free rope is made available to maximize rescue options. The section of rope from the Müenter hitch tie-off at the anchor to the end person (at the anchor) is now available as rescue rope.

b) the middle person has enough rope to reach the lip of the crevasse. If the anchor is placed too far away from the crevasse and the middle does not detach from the rope, this rescuer may be unable to reach the lip to check on the fallen climber.

c) if the best rescue option is to lower the climber to a snowbridge, the middle person can remain near the lip of the crevasse to monitor the lowering. The middle person will be able to stay in position at the lip on self-belay, letting the rope slide through the harness prusik.

Once the anchor has been reinforced, the middle person approaches the crevasse lip on a tight self-belay, as shown in Figure 6-13. Once near the hole, the rescuer should get down on the stomach, crawl forward, and try to establish verbal and visual contact.

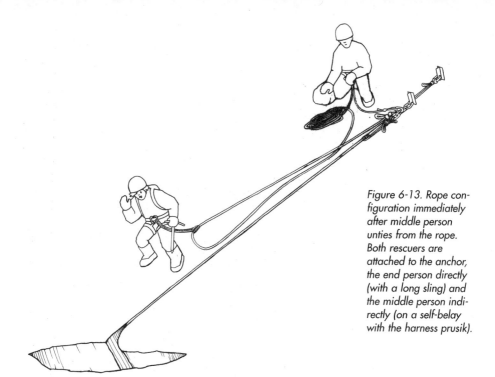

Figure 6-13. Rope configuration immediately after middle person unties from the rope. Both rescuers are attached to the anchor, the end person directly (with a long sling) and the middle person indirectly (on a self-belay with the harness prusik).

The rescuer at the lip should inform the climber that it will take a moment to pad the lip and that it's likely that some snow will be knocked into the crevasse. The object used to pad the lip must be anchored to prevent it from falling into the crevasse. Options for padding the lip are shown in Figure 6-14.

Figure 6-14. Options for padding the crevasse lip. Note that both items are anchored to the slope.

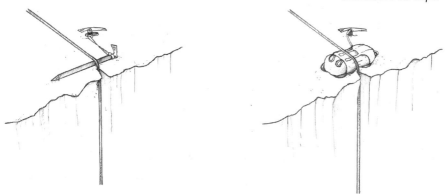

- Step 6—*Select and implement the rescue option.*

You will not know what rescue option to implement until contact has been made with the climber in the crevasse. In the best case scenario, the climber has ascended the rope to the lip and simply needs assistance over the top. At the other extreme, a rescuer may have to rappel into the crevasse to render aid to an unconscious or severely injured person. Whatever the situation, observe these general principles when implementing a rescue:

a) Keep the rescue as simple as possible. Too often rescue teams become so focused on applying a particular system that they overlook a simple solution, such as lowering the fallen climber to a snow ramp for a convenient exit. If a raising rescue is required, it's important to select the one that is best suited to the particular situation; it's essential to know the merits and limitations of the basic systems. Hauling rescues are discussed in detail in following sections.

b) Build systems that can be modified. Construct a base system that can be readily modified if additional mechanical advantage is needed, or if the system needs to be reconfigured. It should be possible to make adjustments to the system without compromising the system's integrity or the team's safety.

c) Make the system reversible. The importance of this principle has already been discussed. In general, avoid using fixed knots (which are impossible to undo under load) when attaching cordelettes, slings, or the rope itself to the anchor. Use tension-release knots to connect any component directly associated with the raising mechanism.

- Step 7—*Tend to the climber.*

Successful closure for any rescue involves more than getting the climber over the lip to safety and administering first aid. The rescuers should take steps to ensure the safety and well-being of the entire team, such as making sure that everyone is attached to an anchor, making food and water available, and safely reconfiguring the rope for travel once the rescue is completed. Depending on the climber's condition, camp may have to be established in the closest safe location. Crevasse rescue can be tiring and time consuming, so it may be necessary to change plans and camp nearby, even if the fallen climber was uninjured.

RESCUE SYSTEMS FOR A ROPE TEAM OF THREE OR MORE

A rope team of three is the minimum number for safe travel by an independent group. Two rescuers with adequate equipment and a basic understanding of crevasse rescue should be able to extricate a fellow team member from a crevasse, whether the fall be by an end person or the middle person in the team. While it might seem that a rescue would be easier to carry out with three or four surface rescuers, larger teams mean that more people need to be organized and managed.

Confusion can dominate the initial moments of the rescue if the team does not have a clear picture of each person's responsibilities. Realistic practice sessions using actual roped travel configurations are essential. When conditions are challenging (e.g., a white-out) or the situation complex (e.g., an uphill rescue), the rescuers will be grateful for every moment

A group of climbers enjoys rescue practice. Diller Glacier, Oregon. Michael Strong photo

spent learning and practicing each of the rescue systems described below. These systems incorporate mechanical advantage to make hauling easier; you may want to review appendix 3 prior to continuing.

Basic Systems: C-Pulley and Z-Pulley Rescues

This section begins with the bread and butter of raising rescues: the c-pulley and z-pulley systems. Every glacier traveler should know how to construct, manage, and modify these basic systems. In most situations, one of these systems will be adequate to implement a rescue. Should one be chosen over the other? In most cases, the c-pulley should be the first choice for raising a fallen climber who cannot ascend the rope but is conscious and able to provide at least some help because:

- *it's the least complex rescue to set up.* The rescue team will have constructed most of the c-pulley by the time one of the rescuers approaches the lip to check on the fallen climber;
- *the fallen climber can assist in the rescue process,* so that less mechanical advantage (hence a less complicated system) is needed;
- *the c-pulley forms the foundation for all other rescues.* It can be easily modified if more mechanical advantage is needed, or the system needs to be reconfigured.

When the climber cannot ascend the rope and is unable to provide any meaningful help due to injuries sustained in the fall, the rescue must be conducted exclusively from the surface of the glacier. The z-pulley is the best choice in this situation. It's fairly easy to set up, modify, and reconfigure if more mechanical advantage is required.

The C-Pulley Rescue

In the c-pulley rescue, a pulley and a locking carabiner are attached to a bight of rope, then lowered to the climber in the crevasse. The climber clips the locking carabiner into the seat harness. The c-pulley is now in place, as shown in Figure 6-15.

The bight of rope has an "anchored" strand and a "haul" strand. While you're pulling on the haul strand, the climber pulls down on the anchored strand. This action partially unweights the climber, lightening the load.

As the climber is hauled up, slack accumulates in the climber's tie-in rope. The rescuer on self-belay removes this rope from the slot it's created (once enough slack develops), and places it over the padded edge. The rescuer at the anchor then pulls the slack through the tension release mechanism on the climbing rope and makes sure that it securely grips the rope. The hauling system is now backed up. You can rest should you need to, and assess the climber's position before beginning another round of hauling.

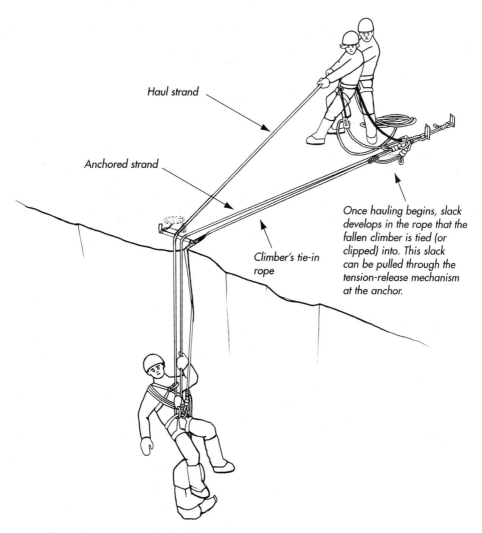

Haul strand

Anchored strand

Climber's tie-in rope

Once hauling begins, slack develops in the rope that the fallen climber is tied (or clipped) into. This slack can be pulled through the tension-release mechanism at the anchor.

Notice that each rescuer is attached to the anchor: The middle is on self-belay with the harness ascender and the end is clipped to the anchor with a long sling.

Figure 6-15. The c-pulley rescue.

Converting the C-Pulley to a Z-Pulley

You may discover that the combined weight of climber and pack may be too heavy to raise with a c-pulley system. Additional mechanical advantage may be required, in which case the c-pulley system can be quickly converted to a z-pulley system as shown in Figure 6-16.

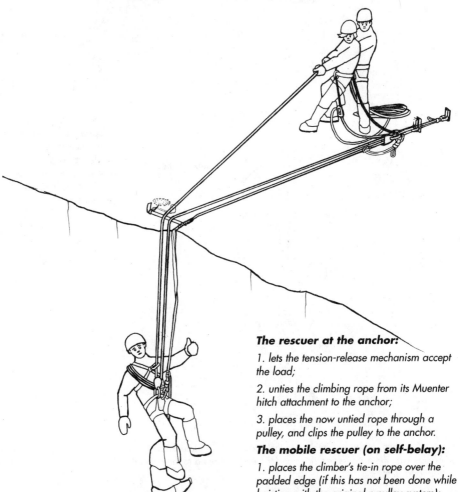

Figure 6-16. Converting a c-pulley to a z-pulley.

The rescuer at the anchor:

1. lets the tension-release mechanism accept the load;

2. unties the climbing rope from its Muenter hitch attachment to the anchor;

3. places the now untied rope through a pulley, and clips the pulley to the anchor.

The mobile rescuer (on self-belay):

1. places the climber's tie-in rope over the padded edge (if this has not been done while hoisting with the original c-pulley system);

2. returns to the anchor to assist with hauling.

The system is now configured into a z-pulley, with the rope running as follows: from the climber up through the pulley at the anchor, back down to the pulley on the climber's harness, and then back up to the rescuers.

Should you want to rest or check the climber's progress at any time, just transfer the load to the tension-release mechanism at the anchor. The mobile rescuer is now free to self-belay to the crevasse lip to talk with the climber or give the climber a helping hand over the lip.

The Z-Pulley Rescue

When the climber in the crevasse cannot offer assistance, there is no sense in even constructing a c-pulley system; it will certainly be inadequate. A better choice in this situation is to immediately build a z-pulley system. It provides more mechanical advantage than a c-pulley and saves time and rescue rope because (in contrast to the converted c-pulley described in the previous section), it is configured entirely on the surface.

Implement the rescue as illustrated and described in Figure 6-17.

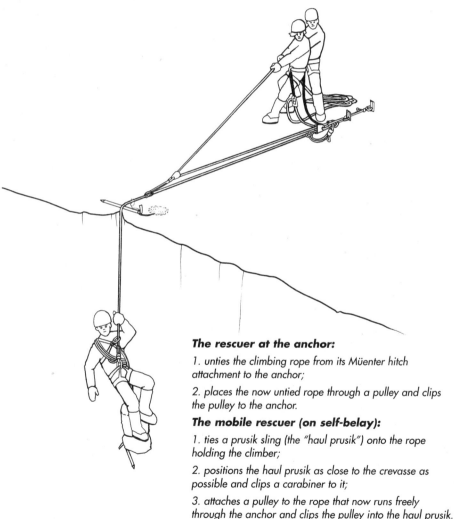

Figure 6-17. The z-pulley system.

The rescuer at the anchor:

1. unties the climbing rope from its Müenter hitch attachment to the anchor;

2. places the now untied rope through a pulley and clips the pulley to the anchor.

The mobile rescuer (on self-belay):

1. ties a prusik sling (the "haul prusik") onto the rope holding the climber;

2. positions the haul prusik as close to the crevasse as possible and clips a carabiner to it;

3. attaches a pulley to the rope that now runs freely through the anchor and clips the pulley into the haul prusik.

The rope is configured into a Z shape, running from the climber up through the pulley at the anchor, back down the pulley on the haul prusik, and then back up to the rescuers.

Once hauling begins, the following sequence of events occurs:

- The tension release mechanism at the anchor is unweighted (Fig. 6-18). Make sure that the incoming rope moves freely through the prusik knot on this mechanism, and that the prusik doesn't jam in the anchor pulley. When a prusik-minding pulley or a pulley with a narrow side span is used, the prusik knot abuts against the pulley and remains in position while the rope moves freely through the system. When a pulley with a wider span is used in combination with a prusik tied from narrow (e.g., 5.5 mm Spectra) cord, the knot may jam. You may have to repeatedly set the prusik down the rope while hauling to prevent it from jamming, a cumbersome task.

- The haul prusik approaches the anchor as the climber is raised (Fig. 6-19). When it is no closer than a foot away from the anchor, stop hauling, so the Z configuration is not compromised. At this point the anchor rescuer "sets" the tension-release mechanism as far down the rope as

Figure 6-18. The tension release mechanism holds the load while the haul prusik is repositioned.

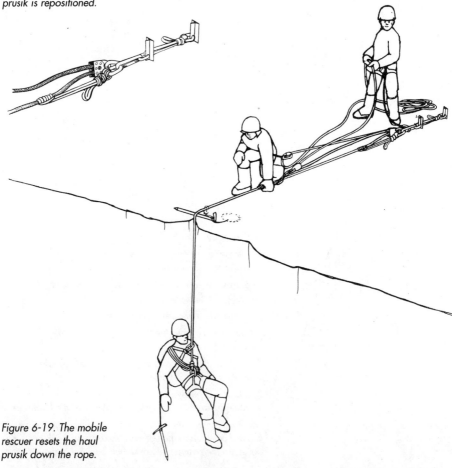

Figure 6-19. The mobile rescuer resets the haul prusik down the rope.

possible and lets it slowly accept the load, as shown in Figure 6-18.

- The mobile rescuer loosens the haul prusik and slides it down the rope toward the crevasse, once again on self-belay (see Fig. 6-19). While near the lip, the mobile rescuer should check on the climber's condition and assess how much raising is left to do. Repeat this sequence until the climber is hoisted to safety.

Hauling without Pulleys

Even when pulleys are used, hoisting can be exhausting. When pulleys are not available and the climber is heavy, you must use every advantage possible to make your task easier. Here are several ways to make hauling easier:

- Use two nonlocking carabiners at each point where pulleys would be used, such as at the anchor and at the haul prusik. Less friction results when the rope runs over two carabiners than over one carabiner.

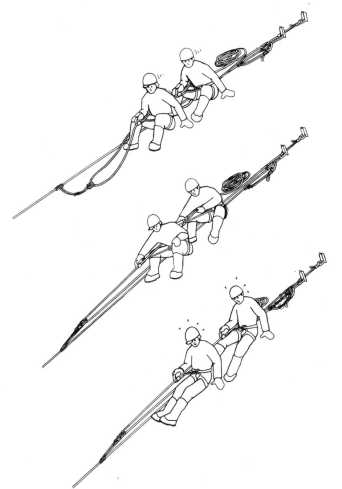

On "forward," scrunch as far forward as you can.

On "ready," slide your harness ascender (or prusik) down the rope as far as possible.

On "heave," lean back and push with your legs.

Figure 6-20. Using the power of the leg muscles to aid in hoisting.

- Sit down and haul in unison, using the strength of the legs to gain additional power. Each rescuer sits in front of the anchor as shown in Figure 6-20, attaches the harness ascender or seat harness prusik to the haul strand (if it's not already positioned on this rope), and clips it into a carabiner on the seat harness. You are now in a position to haul by pushing with the leg muscles, transferring your combined efforts directly from the legs to the rope. You are also in a convenient position to rest during the hauling process.

The following cadence coordinates the hoisting effort. Scrunch as far forward as possible on "forward," slide your friction knots down the rope on "ready," and haul on "heave."

Once hauling begins, make sure that the prusik knot on the tension-release mechanism (at the anchor) (Fig. 6-21A) doesn't slip through the carabiners at the anchor and over to the wrong side of the system (Fig. 6-21B). If the prusik slips to the wrong side, you'll have to reposition it back onto the

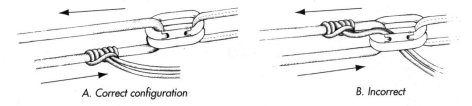

A. Correct configuration   B. Incorrect

Figure 6-21. The tension-release prusik has slipped through the carbiners to the wrong side of the system. Note: In this position the tension-release mechanism cannot hold the load without having to be repositioned.

correct side so that it can hold the load when you reset the haul prusik back down the rope. You will have to lower the climber back down until the knot moves back through the carabiners into its correct orientation, a potentially troublesome task when you're holding the weight of the climber. The knot may jam in the carabiners and then release with a sudden jerk. Be careful!

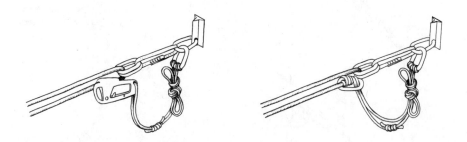

Figure 6-22. A mechanical ascender, left, and a Bachmann knot, right, in the tension-release mechanism.

If you don't have a prusik minding pulley, you can use either a mechanical ascender or a Bachmann knot in the tension release mechanism (Fig. 6-22). Neither will slide through the anchor carabiners. An ascender is an acceptable substitute in this situation, as it will have to hold no more than body weight at any point during the rescue process.

Using a Directional

When crevasses are close together, it's conceivable that a z-pulley will have to be set up from a narrow space between two crevasses. When working space is limited, consider placing a directional and hauling parallel to the crevasse field as shown in Figure 6-23.

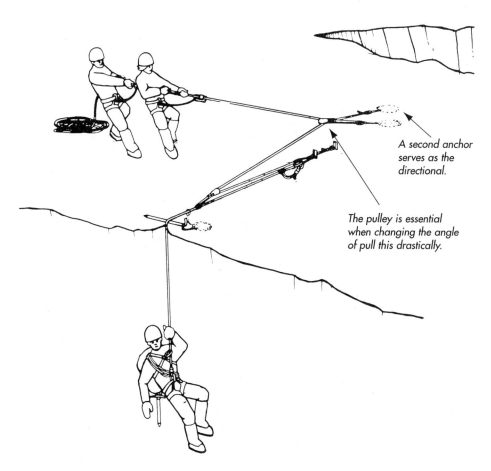

A second anchor serves as the directional.

The pulley is essential when changing the angle of pull this drastically.

Figure 6-23. Hoisting with a directional. The rescuers are attached to the rope via self-belay with the harness ascenders.

Managing an Entrenched Rope

A rope that has cut well into the crevasse lip presents two major problems:

- *Rope drag*—There will probably be a great deal of friction in any hauling system built with an entrenched rope. Also, the rope will saw away once hoisting begins, further embedding it. Padding slipped under the rope will prevent further entrenchment, but will do little to lessen existing friction.

- *Extracting the climber from the crevasse*—The climber will be pulled into, rather than over the crevasse lip if hoisted on a rope that is deeply entrenched in the lip. A climber who's ascending the rope will also find it a difficult, if not impossible, undertaking to get out of the crevasse.

The solution to this predicament is to lower a c-pulley over a freshly padded edge and rescue the climber on this system. But be careful when approaching the lip, because there's probably a very good reason why the rope cut such a deep slot in the first place; it may have sawed into the roof of a snowbridge, or an unstable crevasse lip. You may have to remove a lot of snow from the lip until the true wall of the crevasse is revealed, knocking a fair amount of snow onto the climber in the process.

Once the c-pulley has been lowered, continue with the rescue as previously described.

Recovering after Hoisting a Climber into an Overhang

It is not uncommon to get overzealous during a hauling rescue and haul the climber into, rather than over the crevasse lip. When this happens you must quickly free the climber from this uncomfortable and potentially harmful predicament. Proceed as follows:

If you're hoisting with the *c-pulley* system, lower the climber immediately (Fig. 6-24). You'll be able to do this if you haven't pulled the accumulated slack in the climber's tie-in rope through the tension-release mechanism at the anchor. If you have, there are two options:

- *Option 1:* Haul the climber just enough to take the load off of the tension-release mechanism. A word of caution: You've just pulled the climber into the overhang and any extra hoisting (even the small amount needed to unweight the tension-release mechanism) may produce further discomfort or injury. Find out from the climber if a small amount of additional hoisting is acceptable. If you get the green light, hoist slowly and loosen the tension-release knot as soon as possible. When lowering, make sure the tension-release knot does not accept the load until you're ready for it to do so.

- *Option 2:* If hoisting the climber even the slightest amount is not an option, untie the tension-release mechanism from the anchor and transfer the load onto the rope. Untie the back-up knot (on the rope's Müenter

Figure 6-24. Lowering a wedged climber after hauling with a c-pulley.

hitch tie-off to the anchor) and lower the climber a few feet, using the Müenter hitch as a belay device.

If you hoist the climber into the crevasse roof with a *z-pulley* system (Fig. 6-25) and the tension-release mechanism is not holding any portion of the load (e.g., you're in the middle of a hauling sequence), lower the climber while at the same time making sure the tension-release mechanism doesn't accept any weight. If you've hoisted the climber into the roof and then let the tension-release mechanism at the anchor hold the load (so that the mobile rescuer can go to the edge and check on the climber's predicament), don't hoist any further! Lower the climber on the rope. Once again, you have two options:

- *Option 1:* Transfer the load back onto the haul strand by hoisting just far enough to unweight the tension-release mechanism. See option 1 in the previous section (recovering after hoisting with the c-pulley) for concerns about doing this.

- *Option 2:* Take the rope out of the pulley at the anchor and tie it onto an anchor carabiner with a Müenter hitch. Once the Müenter hitch is in place, loosen (or untie) the tension-release mechanism and lower the climber on the rope.

Figure 6-25. Lowering a wedged climber after hauling with a z-pulley.

Once the climber has been lowered several feet, the mobile rescuer should see if the climber has been injured and inform the climber of the new rescue plan. You may have to hoist the climber out of the crevasse with a c-pulley placed over a newly padded edge, or lower a set of aiders (attached to the rope with prusiks) to help the climber make it over the lip.

Combining Pulley Systems: Solutions for Heavy Hauling

In the great majority of rescue scenarios, a simple c-pulley or z-pulley system will provide more than enough hauling power to assist the climber out of the crevasse. However, there are situations where more power may be required, such as when the rescuers are too tired or weak to raise the load, or rescue pulleys are not available, or when one rescuer is working alone. In situations like these, c-pulley and z-pulley systems can be combined to generate additional pulling power.

Before examining these systems in detail, it is important to emphasize that they should be tried only when there is a proven need for more hauling power. A hauling system with high mechanical advantage is like a car in first gear: lots of power, but a very low speed. Combined systems are powerful but slow, not to mention that additional time, anchors, gear, and rescue rope are required to put it all together.

Combining pulley systems is relatively straightforward: Build a c-pulley or z-pulley system, then build a second system to apply force to the haul strand of the first system.

Adding on to a C-Pulley

C-pulley on a c-pulley—When a c-pulley system does not provide enough mechanical advantage, you can add on another c-pulley. Proceed according to directions in Figure 6-26.

The rescue system constructed in figure 6-26 has a 4:1 (theoretical) mechanical advantage. Hauling is easier, but a lot of rope must be pulled through the system to raise the climber even a little. Specifically, 4 feet of rope passes through the system for every foot of gain. You may run out of hauling room before the fallen climber is out of the crevasse. Should this happen, simply repeat the sequence of events,

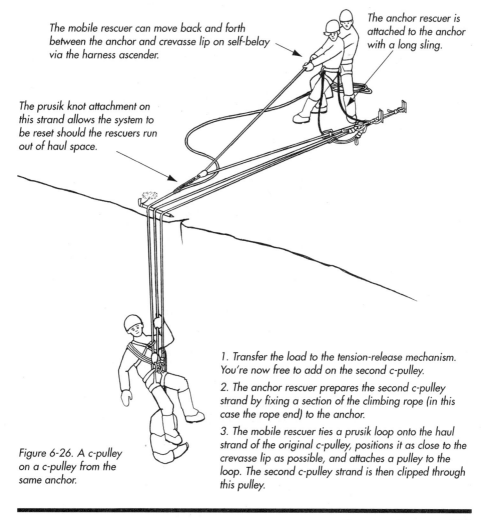

The mobile rescuer can move back and forth between the anchor and crevasse lip on self-belay via the harness ascender.

The anchor rescuer is attached to the anchor with a long sling.

The prusik knot attachment on this strand allows the system to be reset should the rescuers run out of haul space.

Figure 6-26. A c-pulley on a c-pulley from the same anchor.

1. Transfer the load to the tension-release mechanism. You're now free to add on the second c-pulley.

2. The anchor rescuer prepares the second c-pulley strand by fixing a section of the climbing rope (in this case the rope end) to the anchor.

3. The mobile rescuer ties a prusik loop onto the haul strand of the original c-pulley, positions it as close to the crevasse lip as possible, and attaches a pulley to the loop. The second c-pulley strand is then clipped through this pulley.

beginning with transferring the climber's weight to the tension-release mechanism at the anchor in order to reset the haul prusik.

When pulley systems are coupled together, the load on the anchor system is increased. For this reason, some rescuers prefer to build a second anchor behind the first one, and attach the second c-pulley to this anchor (Fig. 6-27). This practice distributes the load between both anchor systems and creates more room to haul.

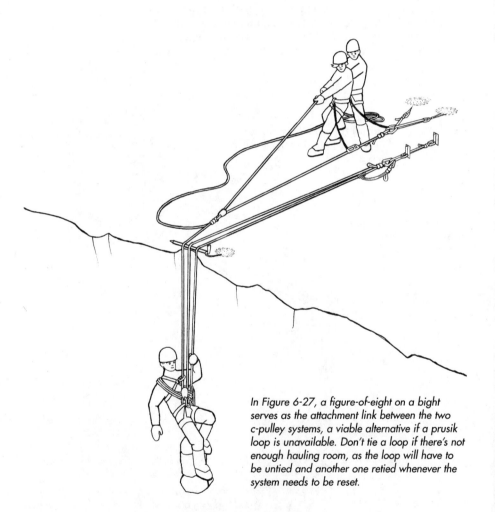

In Figure 6-27, a figure-of-eight on a bight serves as the attachment link between the two c-pulley systems, a viable alternative if a prusik loop is unavailable. Don't tie a loop if there's not enough hauling room, as the loop will have to be untied and another one retied whenever the system needs to be reset.

Figure 6-27. Configuring a c-pulley on a c-pulley from a second anchor.

Z-pulley on a c-pulley—If stacked, or combined, c-pulleys don't provide enough mechanical advantage to do the job, a z-pulley can be added onto the c-pulley system. Once again, a second anchor can be built to increase hauling room or to share the load, as shown in Figure 6-28.

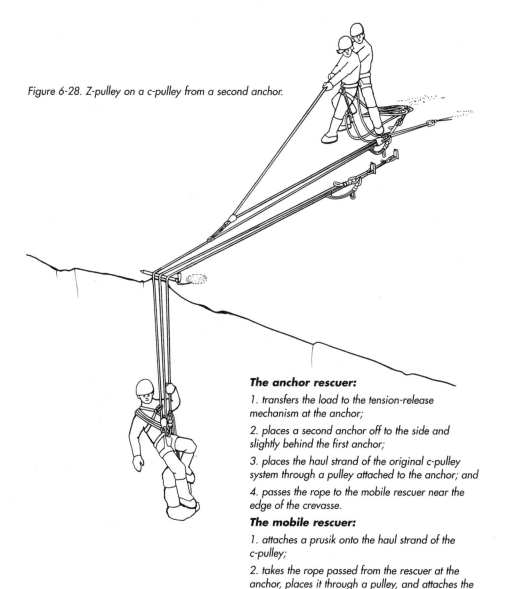

Figure 6-28. Z-pulley on a c-pulley from a second anchor.

The anchor rescuer:

1. transfers the load to the tension-release mechanism at the anchor;

2. places a second anchor off to the side and slightly behind the first anchor;

3. places the haul strand of the original c-pulley system through a pulley attached to the anchor; and

4. passes the rope to the mobile rescuer near the edge of the crevasse.

The mobile rescuer:

1. attaches a prusik onto the haul strand of the c-pulley;

2. takes the rope passed from the rescuer at the anchor, places it through a pulley, and attaches the pulley to the haul prusik.

Adding on to a Z-Pulley

When a z-pulley system doesn't provide enough mechanical advantage, the simplest thing to do is add a c-pulley onto it, as shown in Figure 6-29.

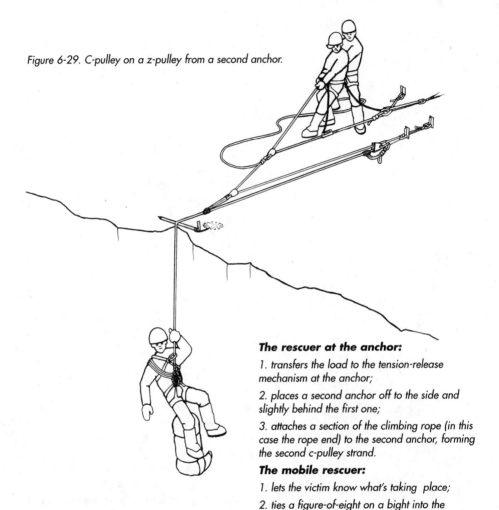

Figure 6-29. C-pulley on a z-pulley from a second anchor.

The rescuer at the anchor:

1. transfers the load to the tension-release mechanism at the anchor;

2. places a second anchor off to the side and slightly behind the first one;

3. attaches a section of the climbing rope (in this case the rope end) to the second anchor, forming the second c-pulley strand.

The mobile rescuer:

1. lets the victim know what's taking place;

2. ties a figure-of-eight on a bight into the climbing rope just above the haul prusik;

3. passes the c-pulley strand through the pulley. The system is configured.

Whenever a c-pulley and a z-pulley are combined, 6 feet of rope move through the system (after rope stretch is removed) for every foot the climber is raised. It's unlikely that you'll be able to raise the climber without having to reset the system several times. To reset the system, transfer the load to the tension-release mechanism, then slide the haul prusik as close to the crevasse edge as possible. The system is now ready for another haul cycle. Take a moment to check on the climber in the crevasse before hauling begins.

A c-pulley on a z-pulley results in the same theoretical mechanical advantage as a z-pulley on a c-pulley (6:1). There are, however, important differences between these two configurations. To begin with, a c-pulley on a z-pulley exerts about 40 percent more stress on the anchor than a z-pulley on a c-pulley. For this reason, it's a good idea to place a second anchor and haul from it as shown in Figure 6-29, rather than hauling with the c-pulley attached to the original anchor. The z-pulley on a c-pulley is not without its disadvantages; it requires a longer strand of rescue rope.

Should conditions be suitable (i.e., bombproof anchor system and enough working space), a c-pulley can be added to a z-pulley from the same anchor, as shown in Figure 6-30.

In this case, the second c-pulley is built by attaching the end of the rope to the anchor.

Figure 6-30. C-pulley on a z-pulley from the same anchor.

Special Problems

Not all rescues are straightforward; events rarely unfold exactly as planned. There will come a time when a rescue stretches the limits of the team, and demands a higher degree of improvisation and creative problem solving than has already been discussed. Uphill rescues, rescues conducted with limited working space, and middle person falls can be particularly challenging. The rope team intent on passing through heavily crevassed terrain in less than ideal surface conditions has the highest chance of encountering one of these difficult rescue situations; extra time on the practice slope is definitely in order before the team sets out.

The Bilgeri Rescue

The Bilgeri rescue is best described as a team self-rescue. Rather than the climber ascending unassisted out of the crevasse, a set of friction knots is managed by a rescuer at the anchor. The Bilgeri system is ideal for a climber who cannot work with prusiks (e.g., cold hands), is very inexperienced, or is otherwise having difficulty ascending. It is also ideal in situations where the rope has cut a deep slot in the lip. Because the prusik knots are manipulated from above, there are no knots for the climber to work up through the slot and over the lip. Set up the Bilgeri rescue as illustrated in Figure 6-31.

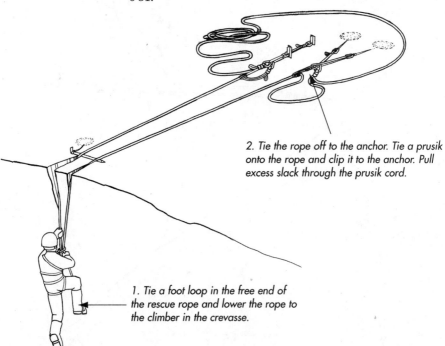

2. Tie the rope off to the anchor. Tie a prusik onto the rope and clip it to the anchor. Pull excess slack through the prusik cord.

1. Tie a foot loop in the free end of the rescue rope and lower the rope to the climber in the crevasse.

Figure 6-31. Setting up the Bilgeri rescue. Note: For clarity a second anchor is shown and the rescuers removed.

The rescuer at the edge of the crevasse coordinates the rescue sequence (Fig. 6-32). On the command "lift" the climber lifts the leg in preparation to weight the foot loop. The rescuer at the anchor takes the slack out of the foot line by pulling it through the prusik at the anchor. The rescuer at the edge then calls "stand" and the climber stands in the foot loop. Slack develops in the climber's tie-in rope. The rescuer at the anchor pulls this slack through the friction knot in the tension release mechanism. On the command "sit" the climber sits down, weighting the tie-in rope. The sequence is repeated and the climber inches slowly upward.

If the tie-in rope has cut a slot so deep that exit from the crevasse is difficult, the climber can clip the foot loop to the seat harness to serve as the support rope while the originally loaded line is loosened (at the tension release mechanism), removed from the slot, and placed over the padded edge. After this transition is complete, the foot loop can be removed from the seat harness and used, once again, as a foot loop.

The Bilgeri can also be implemented when the climber is carrying a heavy pack; however, the climber must remove the pack and detach from the rope (or vice versa depending on the pack tethering system used). The harness ascender now serves as the climber's attachment to the rope. With every step up in the foot loop, slack develops in the harness ascender cord. It's best that the climber remove this slack by sliding the ascender up the rope rather than having the rescuer at the anchor pull this slack through the tension release knot at the anchor. Why? Because the rescuer will have to raise the pack with every pull, a difficult undertaking if rope friction over the edge is excessive.

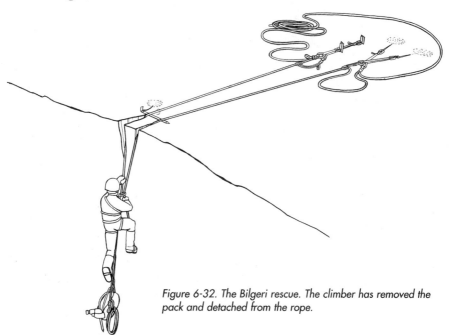

Figure 6-32. The Bilgeri rescue. The climber has removed the pack and detached from the rope.

So, what's the point of using a Bilgeri when a heavy pack has to be managed? Perhaps the climber has rigged with a harness ascender and a foot prusik and cannot work the foot prusik effectively. Or perhaps the climber did not pre-rig the foot prusik and dropped it while dangling on the rope. If uninjured the climber will be able to easily slide the harness ascender up the rope.

Another advantage of the Bilgeri system is that no heavy hauling is required. This can be a critical advantage if the people carrying out the rescue from above lack the necessary strength, are injured, or don't know how to establish a hauling system. In soft snow, the ropes don't cut into the crevasse edge as much as they are under less tension while being pulled.

Lack of Working Space

A serious situation occurs when for some reason (lack of alertness, slack in the rope, or weight of the fallen climber) the surface team is dragged for some distance before holding the fall. When the fall is eventually contained, the middle person may be so close to the edge of the crevasse that it's not

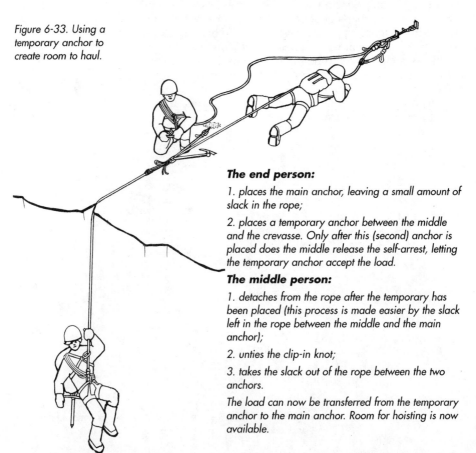

Figure 6-33. Using a temporary anchor to create room to haul.

The end person:

1. places the main anchor, leaving a small amount of slack in the rope;

2. places a temporary anchor between the middle and the crevasse. Only after this (second) anchor is placed does the middle release the self-arrest, letting the temporary anchor accept the load.

The middle person:

1. detaches from the rope after the temporary has been placed (this process is made easier by the slack left in the rope between the middle and the main anchor);

2. unties the clip-in knot;

3. takes the slack out of the rope between the two anchors.

The load can now be transferred from the temporary anchor to the main anchor. Room for hoisting is now available.

possible to set an anchor, much less build a rescue system between this person and the edge, as one would ordinarily do. It seems logical in this situation to have the end person place the anchor at a point behind the middle person and build a rescue system from this anchor. Unfortunately, the middle person would then remain trapped under tension as soon as the weight is transferred to this anchor. An alternate solution is illustrated in Figure 6-33.

Uphill Rescues

Uphill rescues (Figs. 6-34 through 6-37) can be very demanding because the rescuers must fight gravity at every step. It's often easier and safer to rescue the climber from the downhill side of the crevasse. Usually, the hardest part of this process is relocating the surface team safely to the downhill side.

- Step 1—*Place an anchor and check on the fallen climber.* The middle holds the load while you self-belay down the slope, place an anchor between the middle and the crevasse, and transfer the load to it in the usual fashion. The middle releases from self-arrest and self-belays to the lip to check on the climber. In this scenario, let's assume that the climber cannot ascend the rope and, that given the steepness of the slope, you decide to move the rescue to the downhill side of the crevasse. Tell the climber in the crevasse of your decision, and ask if he/she feels capable of clipping a loop of rope to the seat harness. If the answer is yes, proceed (the reason for this will become clear in a moment).

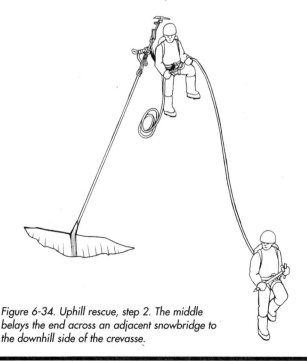

Figure 6-34. Uphill rescue, step 2. The middle belays the end across an adjacent snowbridge to the downhill side of the crevasse.

- Step 2—*Cross to the downhill side of the crevasse.* The middle attaches to the anchor system with a long sling and removes the tie-in knot from the rope, making as much rope as possible available for the crossing. Carefully find a way across the crevasse, belayed by the middle (Fig. 6-34).

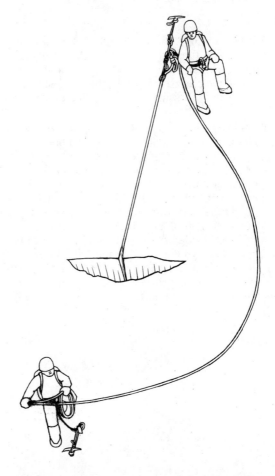

Figure 6-35. Uphill rescue, step 3. The downhill rescuer reels in excess rope after being belayed to the downhill side. Note the sling attachment to the anchor.

- Step 3—*Transfer the climber onto the downhill anchor.* While still on belay, place a solid anchor on the downhill side, well back from the edge of the crevasse. Attach to the anchor with a long sling and then call "off belay" to your partner. Pull the slack out of the rope between you and the middle (the uphill rescuer) and attach it to the anchor with a tension-release mechanism. At this point the rope runs from the fallen climber up to the uphill anchor, and then to the downhill anchor (Fig. 6-35).

Tie a loop in the end of the rope and attach a locking carabiner to it. Proceed to the edge on self-belay (Fig. 6-36A) and lower the carabiner to the climber in the crevasse (figure 6-36B). Instruct the climber to clip the carabiner to the seat harness and lock it. If possible, have the uphill rescuer monitor this process from the uphill edge of the crevasse, confirming

A   B   C

The downhill rescuer approaches the lip and lowers a rescue loop (with locking carabiner attached) to the climber.

The climber clips the rope lowered from the downhill side into the seat harness.

After clipping into the rope lowered from the downhill side, the climber unclips from the rope running to the uphill side (the original clip-in rope).

The climber is now safely transferred to the downhill rope.

Figure 6-36. Uphill rescue, step 3, continued.

that the fallen climber has attached, and secured the locking carabiner. As soon as the climber is clipped in, take the slack out of the rope you just lowered at the tension release mechanism on the downhill anchor. The uphill rescuer lowers the climber off of the original anchor until the weight is transferred to the new downhill rope. The climber is now free to detach from the (now) slack rope running to the uphill side (Fig. 6-36C).

- Step 4—*Belay the middle to the downhill side.* As soon as the climber has been transferred to the downhill rope,

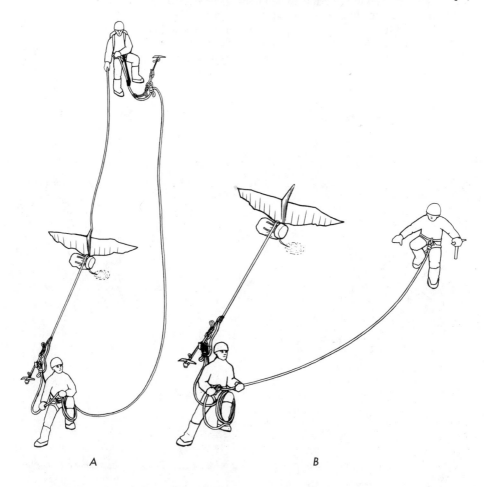

A   B

The climber has been transferred to the downhill anchor. The uphill rescuer pulls the rope out of the crevasse and ties into the end of it.

The downhill rescuer belays the uphill rescuer to the downhill side.

Figure 6-37. Uphill rescue, step 4.

the uphill rescuer pulls the climber's original tie-in rope out of the crevasse and ties into it. After making the necessary safety adjustments, the uphill rescuer removes the anchor and gives you the signal to belay for the crossing to the downhill side (Fig. 6-37).

- Step 5—*Hoist the climber out of the crevasse.* Once you're reunited with the middle, rescue the climber with an appropriate hauling system.

Events, of course, may conspire to prevent you from rescuing the climber exactly as described. It may not be safe, or even possible to reach the downhill side, there may not be adequate rescue rope to make the downhill transition, and so on. If such obstacles impede you, either find a way to overcome them, or proceed with an uphill rescue.

Rescuing the Middle Person

Falls by the middle person are unusual. If a snowbridge is going to break, it will usually break under the weight of the leader. Because of this, many climbers devote much of their practice time to rescuing an end person, and do not give middle person falls much thought. This is unfortunate, considering the added complexities that a fall by the middle person can create.

A fall by the middle person presents special challenges: The surface rescuers are separated by a greater distance, making communication difficult, especially while face-first in self-arrest. Even if communication is good, who's going to set up the anchor? What if the terrain won't allow the rescuers to join forces? Can one rescuer generate enough power to haul the climber from the crevasse? And what about the fallen climber? On which rope should the middle person try to ascend?

Let's answer these questions by observing how a rope team of three climbers works through the rescue sequence.

With Erica in front, Dana in the middle, and Andy trailing, the team makes its way out of their wanded camp, on the final push to the base of the mountain's upper slopes. Crevasses are hard to detect due to a fresh blanket of snow. As the team works up a gentle slope, Erica comes to a partially exposed crevasse with several snowbridges. Choosing the one that appears strongest, she crosses with no trouble. Dana, following behind, is not so fortunate. The bridge collapses beneath him.

- Step 1—*Erica and Andy hold the fall.* Erica and Andy have no problem holding Dana. Each of them was ready for it. From their positions in self-arrest, Andy and Erica have a difficult time hearing each other. They are fairly far apart, separated by most of the rope's length. It's clear to each of them (without saying anything) that Erica took the brunt of the fall. Erica yells to Andy that she's holding all of the weight and that from her uphill position feels quite unstable. Andy, in the meantime, knows that Erica is holding the load and reacts correctly by tensioning the rope between him and Dana as much as possible and reinforcing his stance. He yells to Erica that he's set to accept the load and for her to reinforce her position. Relaxing slowly, Erica lets Andy take the load, then reinforces her self-arrest.

The situation is now stable with the load evenly distributed. Now, who places the anchor? There are several factors to weigh in this decision:

Pulling power. Ideally, the rescuers can reunite so that both can contribute hauling power to any rescue effort. But this may not be possible; the crevasse may be too wide to cross or too long to circumvent, requiring that the rescuers remain on their respective sides. All other factors being equal (skill, experience, etc.), the primary anchor should be set by the climber who's most capable of pulling off a solo rescue.

Terrain. Because it's harder to haul from an uphill position than a downhill one, on steep slopes it's preferable to set the anchor and haul from the downhill side.

Gear. If the crevasse is wide, the surface team may not be able to pool rescue gear. In this case, the anchor should be set by the rescuer with the most complete assortment of gear.

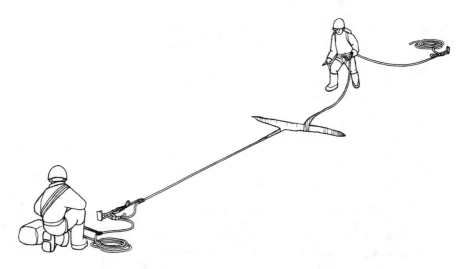

Andy has just placed an anchor allowing Erica to release from self-arrest. After placing the anchor, she is ready to approach the crevasse on self-belay.

Figure 6-38. Middle person rescue, Steps 2-5.

Erica and Andy decide that it's best for Andy to place the anchor because he is stronger, and if Erica can't get over to help him, Andy will have a better chance of hoisting Dana to safety than she will. Also, Erica also does not want to execute an uphill rescue.

- Steps 2 through 4—*Andy places an anchor and transfers the load to it.* Andy slowly releases his self-arrest. Erica holds Dana with no problem. Andy moves quickly into position about 20 feet from the crevasse, places a picket, transfers Dana's load to it and ties the rope off.
- Step 5—*Erica checks on Dana.* Erica releases from self-arrest and immediately places an anchor at her self-arrest site. She then detaches from the rope and clips it to the anchor. On self-belay via her harness prusik, Erica moves towards the crevasse.

What happens next depends on their findings. Several rescue (Step 6) possibilities are presented below.

Scenario 1—Step 6—*Dana is lowered to a snowbridge and climbs out of the crevasse.* Erica reaches the crevasse, lies down, and peeks over the lip. Dana is hanging 20 feet above a snowbridge that ramps up and out of the crevasse. Erica tells Andy to lower Dana to the snowbridge. When Dana lets Erica know he's at the bridge and ready to climb out, she returns to her anchor to get ready to belay him. Belayed by both climbers, Dana exits the crevasse. The team finds a way to reunite themselves (e.g., around the end of the crevasse, another snowbridge, etc.) and continues on their way.

Scenario 2—Step 6—*Dana ascends the rope.* From his position in the crevasse, Dana assesses his situation. With no snow ramp or other easy exit in sight, it seems best to ascend the rope. But which one should he ascend, the one to Andy, or the one to Erica? Making this decision requires a working knowledge of the rescue process; Dana must deduce which rope to ascend based on the few subtle cues available to him.

Checking each rope immediately after the fall, Dana notices that the lead rope is under load, meaning that Erica took the brunt of the fall and is holding him in self-arrest. Will Erica hold the load while Andy places an anchor? It seems likely, since Andy is both the downhill climber and stronger than Erica. But Dana waits and watches: The rope to Erica goes completely slack, then tightens again as the rope to Andy becomes slack. Since it could be disastrous to ascend the wrong rope, Dana decides to wait until he's positive. Eventually Andy's line takes the load again; soon thereafter Erica arrives to check on Dana. He quickly ascends up Andy's line and reaches the surface.

This scenario emphasizes the importance of patience in a middle person fall. No matter how skilled the team is, it is hard to know for *certain* which rope to ascend. Unless there is a very good reason to hurry (for example, imminent hypothermia), it's best to wait.

Scenario 3—Step 6—*Dana is hoisted.* Erica arrives at the lip first and finds Dana hanging at the end of the rope. Wincing in pain and holding his arm against his chest, Dana tells Erica that he's dislocated his shoulder in the fall; he cannot ascend the rope.

Erica lets Andy know that Dana will have to be hauled to the surface. To maximize their pulling power, they first work to get Erica over to Andy's side of the crevasse. While Andy reinforces the main anchor, Erica places yet another anchor on her side, closer to the edge of the crevasse. (Fig. 6-39)

Erica then ties the rope into this anchor, self-belays back to her initial anchor, and removes it. Finally, she returns to her new anchor, clips to it with a long sling, then unties the rope from the anchor and ties into the very end of it. The slack she has created in this transition from one anchor to the other is tossed over to Andy, who puts Erica on belay. There is now enough rope to attempt a belayed crossing (Fig. 6-40).

Erica unclips from the anchor (leaving it in place in case she needs it again) and cautiously moves toward an adjacent snowbridge (Fig. 6-41). Finding the bridge secure, she crosses over to Andy, who clips her into the anchor with enough room for her to assist with the upcoming rescue. Working together, the two rescuers set up a z-pulley and soon have Dana on the surface.

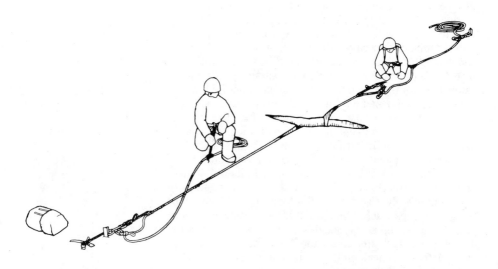

Figure 6-39. Middle person rescue, Scenario 3—Step 6. On self-belay from her original anchor, Erica places a second anchor closer to the crevasse.

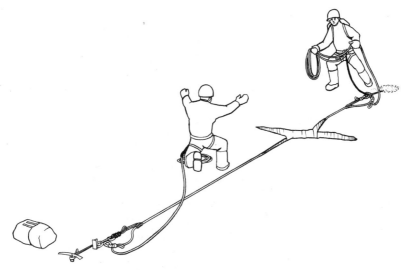

Figure 6-40. Middle person rescue, Scenario 3—Step 6 continued. Erica tosses the rope to Andy in preparation for a belayed crossing.

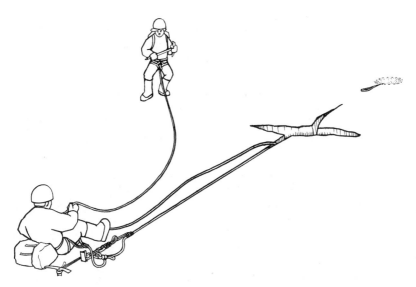

Figure 6-41. Middle person rescue, Scenario 3—Step 6 continued. Andy belays Erica across the snowbridge.

Rescuing the Middle Person: Some Important Considerations

A middle person rescue can be quite complex and require a fair amount of improvisation. Because there are more uncertainties when a middle person goes into a crevasse, it is very important for everyone to have a conceptual understanding of the rescue process and to take into account the following points:

- The middle person should *rig so that either rope can be ascended.* Unlike an end person fall, the climber has to decide which rope to ascend. The climber should always ascend the rope that gets anchored. Of course, the climber will not immediately know which one this is; patience is required. Once the answer is known, the climber should be ready to go with minimal modification to the rigging configuration.

- Unlike an end person fall, *the climber should wait to ascend.* While it may be tempting to ascend one of the ropes immediately, an incorrect decision could have dire consequences. Imagine ascending the rope running to the lone self-arrester, who consequently cannot release from self-arrest to help the fallen climber over the lip.

  If the climber in the crevasse cannot figure out which rope to ascend, it's best to simply wait until clarification is provided from above.

- *Each rescuer must place an anchor* for personal safety and mobility. At no point should either rescuer move about without being attached to an anchor on self-belay. The rescuer coming out of self-arrest must be particularly careful if the decision is made to move back toward the lip to place an anchor. If there's any doubt about the safety of this decision, it's best to place an anchor immediately after getting out of self-arrest. If it's necessary to move closer to the hole to render assistance, it can be done on self-belay from this anchor.

- The *rescuers must know how to couple pulley systems together* in the event that one person has to hoist the middle out alone. When circumstances require that the anchor be built from a specific side, the rescuer placing the anchor should have the resources, skill, and ability to hoist alone.

Scenario 4—*Dana is hoisted by Andy alone.* Erica attempts to cross over the nearby crevasse but can't find a safe crossing point; there is no way for her to join Andy at the main anchor. Erica returns to her anchor, reattaches herself, and assembles a kit of extra rescue gear (her pulley, some extra carabiners, and slings) for Andy. She unties from the end of the rope and clips the gear to it. Andy reels over the gear and continues on, building the rescue system on his own. The most realistic choice, he reasons, is a c-pulley on a z-pulley. Andy knows that Dana cannot assist in the rescue process, making an initial z-pulley necessary. Andy also knows that he won't be able to haul Dana out with just the z-pulley. He'll have to add a c-pulley for additional hoisting power. Andy works diligently and in a short time has the rescue system built. It's tough going, but Dana is slowly raised to the surface.

Rappelling to Aid an Unconscious Climber

Rappelling to help out an unconscious climber is a serious undertaking. When a rescuer goes into a crevasse to render aid, it is with the understanding that without direct and immediate assistance the climber may perish. This is a worst case scenario, one in which the rescue skills of a surface team will be pushed to their limits if no other climbers are available to help.

When it's clear that the climber is unconscious, one rescuer will have to rappel into the crevasse to render aid. If you cannot establish visual contact, and repeated yells elicit no response, waste no time getting into the crevasse.

Unless you're carrying an additional rope or there's another rope immediately available from another rope team, one rope will have to be used for rappelling as well as for hoisting. And since one of you must remain with the climber at all times, the lone surface rescuer must be able to generate enough hauling power alone. This means building a z-pulley and then knowing how to convert it to a more powerful system once more rope becomes available (i.e., the climber is raised a little).

Begin by placing a separate rappel anchor, slightly off to the side and closer to the crevasse than the main anchor. Tie a stopper knot onto the free end of the rope (to prevent rappelling off the end), lower the rope no farther than the climber's feet, and pad the edge (for both ropes). Tie the rappel rope off to the anchor. Figure 6-42 illustrates the rope configuration to this point in the rescue sequence.

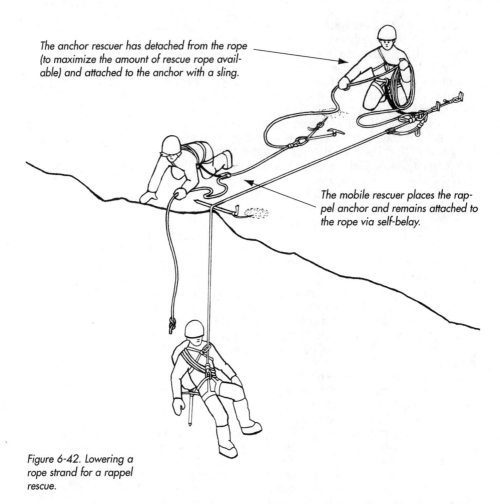

The anchor rescuer has detached from the rope (to maximize the amount of rescue rope available) and attached to the anchor with a sling.

The mobile rescuer places the rappel anchor and remains attached to the rope via self-belay.

Figure 6-42. Lowering a rope strand for a rappel rescue.

What if you cannot see the climber? How will you know how much rescue rope to lower? Remember, you must not waste rope, as you still have to build at least a z-pulley. In this situation every foot of rope counts. You can use the rope's middle as a benchmark; hopefully the middle is marked. For example, if the strand holding the climber is tied off to the main anchor 20 feet from the middle of the rope, then you can tie the rope off to the rappel anchor 20 feet on other side from the middle. The remaining free end (the eventual rappel line) should be the same length as the strand holding the injured climber, leaving you enough length to reach the climber. In this case, 40 feet of rope is made available to haul with; this should be plenty (Fig. 6-43; for clarity, the rescuers are not shown).

While constructing the haul system, take stock of what might be needed: a first-aid kit, extra warm clothing, prusiks, and any carabiners and slings that can be spared. When

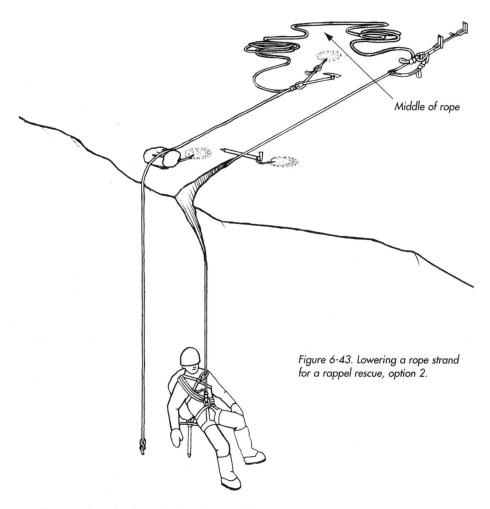

Middle of rope

Figure 6-43. Lowering a rope strand for a rappel rescue, option 2.

ready, rappel on back-up belay via your harness ascender. When you're at eye level with the climber, let your ascender support your weight. For safety, tie the rappel off at your harness.

Immediately check to see if the climber is breathing. When you've confirmed breathing, continue with a secondary assessment. Perform whatever first aid is required, then rig the climber for hoisting.

Your first task is to get the climber into an upright position for raising. Tie a prusik sling on the fallen climber's rope and slide it well above the head. Next, clip a long sling to the attachment point on the climber's chest harness, clip it into a carabiner attached to the prusik and then tie a foot loop into the other end. Stand in the loop, rotating the climber into an upright position. Then clip the climber's chest harness to the prusik carabiner (Fig. 6-44).

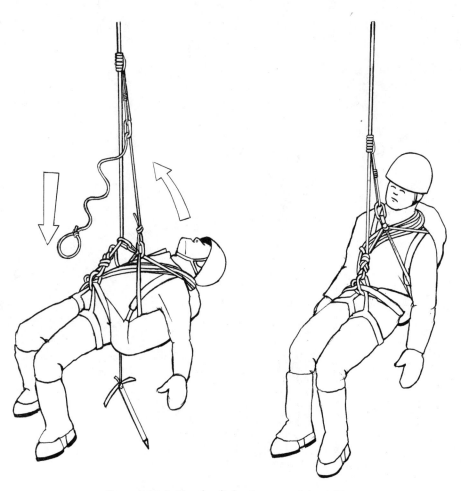

Figure 6-44. Raising the climber into an upright position.

The climber is now upright, and can be rotated up or down (for comfort) by sliding the prusik loop up or down on the rope. The climber's head may also need to be stabilized. You could attach a sling to either side of the helmet, and clip the ends to the prusik sling. If the climber was not wearing a helmet, you could place a doubled sling behind the (padded) head and clip it into the prusik.

Yell to the surface rescuer that the climber is stabilized, and to start hoisting. You're going to have to help, because even the strongest rescuer will not be able to raise both of you with just a z-pulley. You can assist by taking a little of the climber's weight while ascending the rappel rope, as follows:

- Attach a prusik sling to the rappel rope and clip a carabiner to the sling.
- Attach the long sling (just used to rotate the climber into an upright position) to the climber's seat harness and clip

it through the carabiner in the prusik sling on the rappel rope.

- Slide the prusik on the rope until the foot loop is in a convenient position.
- When the surface rescuer yells "pulling," stand upright in the foot loop, partially unweighting the climber, and in the process making it easier to raise the load (Fig. 6-45).

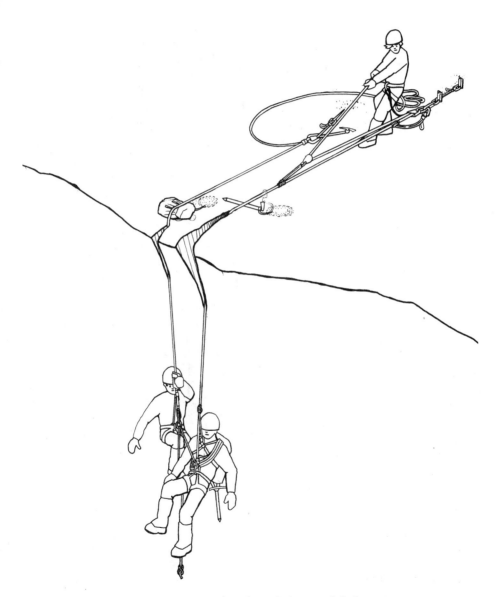

Figure 6-45. Ascending alongside the injured climber.

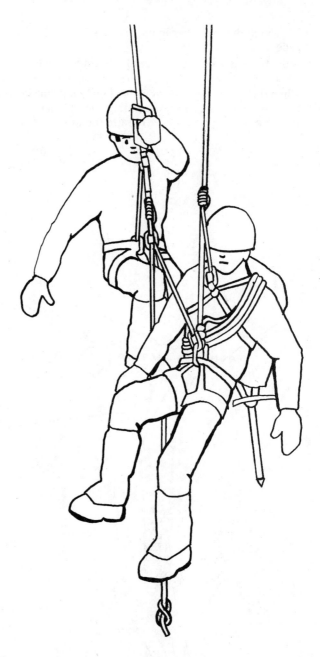

Figure 6-46. Assisting
with the hoisting effort.

If hauling is too difficult (even with your help), the surface rescuer can add a c-pulley to the z-pulley system. There may not be enough rope for this addition early in the rescue, but more rope becomes available as the climber is raised.

Needless to say, it will take a while to raise the climber up, for you also have to ascend the rappel rope. Once the climber is at the lip, the surface rescuer leaves the anchor to help get the climber over the edge.

Rescuing a Climber Pulling a Sled

On long trips over big glaciers, it's not uncommon for at least one climber to be pulling a sled. Just as there are special considerations for rigging and traveling with a sled, there are factors that the rescue team must consider when rescuing someone who has fallen into a crevasse with one.

A climber who cannot ascend past a sled will have to be hauled out on a rope lowered from above. Once the climber has attached this rope to the seat harness and is hoisted a little, the original fall rope can be detached. The climber can then be hoisted on the new rope, free of the sled. The sled can then be retrieved after the fallen climber has been attended to (Fig. 6-47).

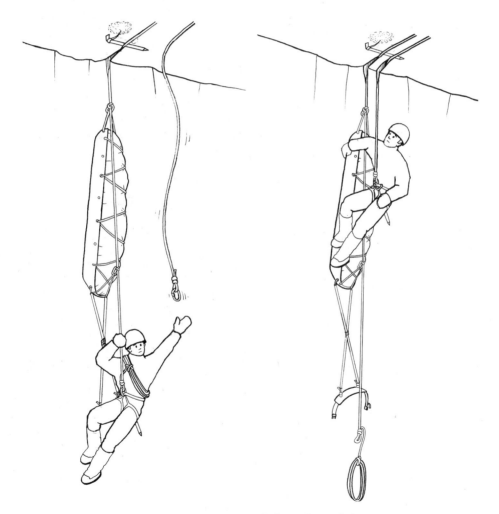

Figure 6-47. Rescuing a climber pulling a sled.

Two rope teams of two approach the greater icefall, Muldrow Glacier, Denali.
Michael Strong photo

RESCUE SYSTEMS FOR A TWO-PERSON ROPE TEAM

There are many reasons to climb with just one other person. It's faster, more personal, and, while on the glacier, a rope team of two is certainly more mobile. However, there are inherent risks associated with two-person independent travel that you should be aware of. To begin with, when your partner falls into a crevasse, you'll be faced with the demanding task of holding the self-arrest, and then placing an anchor from a potentially unstable position. Careful preparation (and some luck) increases the chance that the anchor(s) you need will be accessible and not out of reach, buried in the pack, or wedged underneath you! Even so, you'll have to hoist the climber out of the crevasse without assistance.

This whole process can be an exercise in desperation for an unprepared and underskilled climber. There is absolutely no margin for error in two-person travel. The team intent on traveling independently, especially through technical terrain, must weigh the consequences of this decision very carefully and should practice their rescue systems ahead of time.

The Lone Rescuer or Candian Drop Loop System

An effective system for two-person rescue is the lone rescuer drop loop system, built with a z-pulley on a c-pulley. This system provides enough mechanical advantage (6:1, theoretically), for one person to hoist another out of a crevasse.

The basic idea behind the drop loop system is simple: Drop a c-pulley to your partner and add a z-pulley onto it. An extra-long rescue coil is required to do this without having to modify the system midrescue. When climbers space themselves the minimum recommended distance of 40 feet apart, each end coil must approach 80 feet in length, as shown in Figure 6-48.

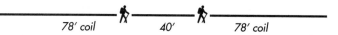

78′ coil   40′   78′ coil

Figure 6-48. Rope configuration for two-person travel. End coil lengths for two-person travel on a 196-foot rope—no knots in the rope.

This rope configuration is definitely not suited for a two-person team traveling on a glacier with wide crevasse spans. On the larger Alaskan-sized glaciers, increase your spacing and travel with at least one other rope team (see chapter 3).

To accommodate long end coils, you must travel on a 60-meter rope. When traveling on a 50-meter rope with a 40-foot spacing arrangement, each end coil will be no more than about 62.5 feet, not quite enough to build the drop loop system.

Even with a system incorporating a 6:1 mechanical advantage, hoisting will be grueling work, as demonstrated in the following scenario.

Erica and Andy have decided to attempt a route on the north face of Mount Hood. They set out onto the Eliot Glacier with Andy in the lead. A short time later Andy disappears into a crevasse without warning.

- Step 1—*Erica holds the fall.* Erica is dragged several feet before she's able to contain Andy's fall. She yells to him from her position in self-arrest. She listens carefully, yet hears nothing.
- Steps 2 through 4—*Erica places an anchor, transfers the load to it, and reinforces the anchor.* Erica must place an anchor while holding her self-arrest. Fortunately, she's positioned a picket in an accessible place: in the wand pocket of her pack. Still, the picket must be driven in somehow. Erica reinforces her stance by kicking her toes solidly into the snow. Keeping her self-arrest grip on the head of the ice axe, Erica turns slowly onto her side, weighting the shaft of the axe with her torso. From this somewhat precarious (and contorted) position, Erica manages to drive the picket into the snow with her second tool, which was holstered on her harness.

After the picket is in place, Erica pulls the tail end of her foot prusik out of her pocket and ties it into the anchor with a Müenter hitch. She slowly releases the self-arrest and lets the tension release cordelette (foot prusik) hold the load. She detaches from her harness prusik (attached to the loaded rope), unties from the rope, clips herself to the anchor with her daisy chain, and clears her tie-in knot. There's now enough slack available to back up the tension-release cordelette as usual (by securing the rope to the anchor with a tied-off Müenter hitch). Erica immediately backs up the first anchor point with a tensioned backup, using her ice axe.

• Step 5—*Erica checks on Andy and pads the edge.* Erica stacks the rescue coils, ties her harness prusik onto the rescue strand, and self-belays to the lip to check on Andy.

• Step 6—*Erica hoists Andy.* Arriving at the edge, Erica finds that Andy has twisted his right knee and injured his left ankle. He's medically stable, but unable to ascend out of the crevasse. Erica will have to rescue Andy with a rescue system that has enough mechanical advantage: the lone rescuer drop loop system.

Erica ties two figure-of-eight loops into the rescue strand, positioning them as far away from the anchor as terrain allows and close together. Erica ties a loop in the free end of the rescue rope and clips it to the loop closest to the anchor. At this point the rescue strand forms one long section from the Müenter hitch at the anchor, back around to the end Erica will clip to the loop closest to the anchor, as shown in Figure 6-49.

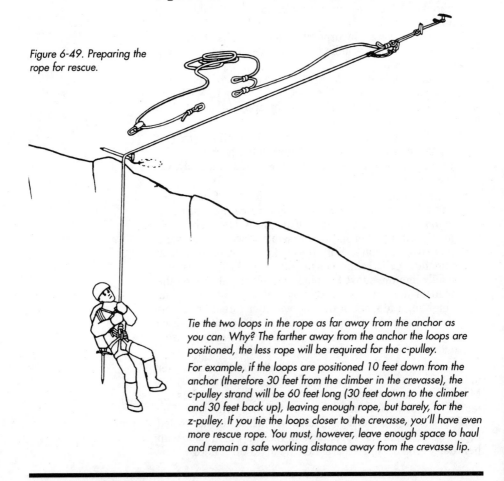

Figure 6-49. Preparing the rope for rescue.

Tie the two loops in the rope as far away from the anchor as you can. Why? The farther away from the anchor the loops are positioned, the less rope will be required for the c-pulley.

For example, if the loops are positioned 10 feet down from the anchor (therefore 30 feet from the climber in the crevasse), the c-pulley strand will be 60 feet long (30 feet down to the climber and 30 feet back up), leaving enough rope, but barely, for the z-pulley. If you tie the loops closer to the crevasse, you'll have even more rescue rope. You must, however, leave enough space to haul and remain a safe working distance away from the crevasse lip.

Erica attaches a pulley to the rescue strand, returns to the lip, and lowers the pulley to Andy, who attaches the pulley to his seat harness. Erica goes back to the anchor and clips two carabiners into the second loop (the one farthest from the anchor). She then takes the section of the rescue strand returning from the pulley in Andy's harness, and clips it through the two carabiners with a Garda knot (see Fig. A1-26 in appendix 1). Finally, Erica attaches a haul prusik to the rope and clips the strand exiting the Garda knot through the carabiner(s) in the haul prusik. The system is configured (see Fig. 6-50).

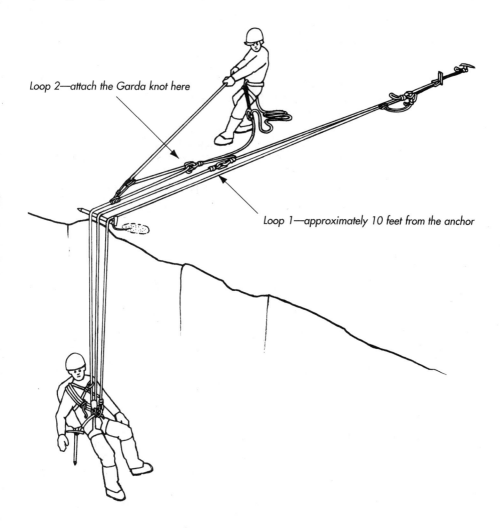

Loop 2—attach the Garda knot here

Loop 1—approximately 10 feet from the anchor

Figure 6-50. The lone rescuer or Canadian drop loop system.

Erica raises Andy with the 6:1 system. Andy helps by pulling down on the anchored strand of the c-pulley. As Andy is raised, slack develops in the original fall rope. Erica pauses occasionally to pull this slack through the tension release knot at the anchor. This is an easy task because the Garda knot locks the haul rope in place after every pull. Throughout the hoisting process Erica periodically resets the haul prusik back farther down the rope. Once again, the one-way locking action of the Garda knot facilitates this process.

• Step 7—*Erica tends to Andy.*

Completely exhausted by her efforts, Erica finally hauls Andy to the lip and wrestles him onto the surface. Although his knee and ankle are tender, he's confident that a tape job will provide the stability he needs to hobble back to the parking lot. After some food, water, and rest, the climbers reconfigure the rope and head home.

Increasing the Efficiency of the Lone Rescuer Drop Loop System

Unless you are extremely strong or your partner very light, you will have a very hard time pulling someone out of a crevasse on your own. There are several ways to increase the efficiency of the drop loop system:

• Lower just the bight of rope and request that your partner attach his/her own locking carabiner and pulley to the rope strand. Use your pulley in the z-pulley segment to reduce friction when hauling.

• Although the Garda knot enables you to hoist without the worry of managing an anchor prusik, it creates a great deal of friction. If you're light and don't relish the prospect of having to hoist a much heavier partner, use a prusik minding pulley in place of the Garda. You will have to add an anchor prusik to hold the load while you reset the z-pulley system during the hoisting sequence. Keep this prusik very short so that it grabs right away when the load is transferred onto it between hoists. Don't forget to add a prusik minding pulley and short prusik cord to your rescue kit.

Other Considerations for Two-Person Rescue

The lone rescuer drop loop system is by no means the only rescue system available to the two-person rope team. For example, you could build the z-pulley first, then add the c-pulley onto it. It's a simpler system to build and does not require such a long rescue coil (making it attractive to climbers with 50-meter ropes). Although this rescue system provides the same theoretical mechanical advantage as the drop loop system (6:1), there is one important difference: it does not enlist the help of the fallen climber. The benefit of having your partner pull on the anchored strand of the c-pulley while you hoist with a z-pulley extension should not be underestimated, especially when you're the lighter and weaker member of the team.

Regardless of the rescue system you prefer, during two-person independent travel it is imperative that:

- you do not travel more than 40 feet apart on glaciers with small crevasse spans (to maximize rescue rope carried in end coils).
- you incorporate a rescue coil that is long enough to rappel into a crevasse;
- you have enough rescue rope to couple pulley systems together (whether it be a c-pulley on a z-pulley or vice versa);
- both climbers mutually agree on the rope configuration for rigging and rescue, and are physically capable and skilled enough to pull off a rescue without help.
- you understand and accept the risks associated with this choice.

Let's say that Andy sustains a serious enough injury during the crevasse fall that he does not respond to Erica's repeated shouts from above. What should Erica do? Her first priority is to rappel into the crevasse, check on Andy's condition and render whatever aid is necessary. Hopefully, Andy is not seriously injured, enabling Erica to tend to his injuries and then attach the c-pulley to his harness before ascending the rope back to the surface.

But what if Andy is seriously injured? What are Erica's options when nobody else is around to help? If Andy's injuries are stable enough to permit Erica to ascend the rope to the surface, she may be strong enough to hoist Andy with a z-pulley on a c-pulley. She may not be. And even if Erica can manage to raise Andy, she'll have an extremely difficult time getting his inert weight over the lip. She probably would not be able to if there's a roof to negotiate. It could very easily be a grim situation without an easy solution.

The moral of such morbid contemplations is worth emphasizing once again: Think very carefully about the risks versus your team's skills and experience before stepping onto a glacier with just one other person and nobody else in sight. Yes, the benefits of traveling with just one partner can outweigh the limitations, especially when you want them to. At least think about the consequences of this decision before making it. As a wise mountaineer once said, judgment does not necessarily come from experience, it comes from experiences that are the result of bad judgment.

The team—in great shape after all those falls and rescues.

APPENDIX 1 Knots for Glacier Travel and Rescue

KNOT SELECTION AND CARE

The glacier traveler has a large selection of knots to choose from. It may be tempting to learn as many knots as possible, but it's usually better to learn the handful of knots essential to a specific situation, and learn them well enough to tie efficiently in demanding conditions. Practice tying knots behind the back with gloves or mittens on, or even in the shower with the lights off!

When it comes to knot selection, ask yourself what *kind* of knot is needed? There are three kinds to choose from: bends, loops, and hitches.

Bends, Loops, and Hitches

Bends join two ends of a rope together. Examples include the ring (overhand; Fig. A1-1) and Flemish (figure-of-eight; Fig. A1-2) bends.

Figure A1-1. Ring bend.

Figure A1-2. Flemish bend.

Bends are easily identified, as the ends come out opposite sides of the knot. Bends are commonly used in glacier travel to tie accessory cord or tubular webbing into *slings* or *runners*.

Loops can be tied two different ways. The method used depends on the circumstance. When tying into the end of the rope, for example, there's no choice but to tie the loop with a *follow-through*. Likewise, a loop tied in the middle of a rope must be tied on a *bight* (Fig. A1-3). Whichever of these two kinds of knots you tie, the finished product looks the same, as shown below.

Figure A1-3. Figure-of-eight follow-through/figure-of-eight on a bight.

Hitches are adjustable knots. Rope can be fed back and forth through a hitch while it remains tied. The Müenter hitch is shown in Figure A1-4.

Performance Qualities

Once you know what kind of knot is needed, selection can be narrowed to one or two knots that will do the job. The choice of one knot over another is best based on a blend of the following performance qualities.

Strength is usually the first quality that comes to mind when deciding on which knot to use. Although it is important, strength should not be the sole determinant for selecting a knot. Knots used by climbers rarely break, largely because the materials used in the construction of ropes, webbing, and accessory cord are more than strong enough to meet the demands normally placed upon them.

Knot *security* is critical. The ability of a knot to stay tied is probably more important than knot strength. Does this mean that the most secure knot is the most appropriate one? Not at all. If this were the case, more climbers would use the overhand follow-through as a tie-in knot. It's certainly strong enough, and it's easier to tie than the figure-of-eight follow-through. The overhand knot, however, is extremely difficult to untie once firmly loaded.

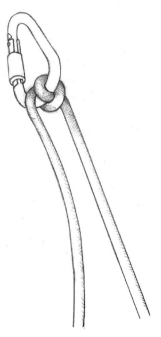

Figure A1-4. Müenter hitch.

Ease of tying is also important. There is no point in choosing a complicated knot when a less complex one will work just as well. *Ease of untying after loading* is especially important with gloves or mittens on, or if the rope is wet or icy.

Ease of visual inspection is a performance quality that should not be overlooked. It's important to be able to glance at the tie-in or clip-in knots of rope team members, or the knots of a rescue system and quickly recognize whether these knots are tied correctly.

One way to evaluate whether the right kind of knot has been selected for the job is to examine the knot when it's loaded. Look to see if the knot is *stressed along its long axis.* If it isn't (e.g., the stress is sideways), the knot may be split apart under load, compromising its strength and security (Figs. A1-5 and A1-6).

Figure A1-5. A knot stressed along its long axis—correct application.

Figure A1-6. A knot stressed sideways across its long axis—incorrect application.

Knot Management

A knot must be *dressed,* or tied in its most secure orientation. In most knots tied with accessory cord, this means making sure that strands running side by side through a knot do not cross. Knots with crossed strands may not snug together, can jam badly, and pose the risk of coming loose.

The manner in which knots are dressed may be quite different, so know how to efficiently dress each knot. For example, the butterfly knot is dressed by loosely tying the knot and then pulling the rope strands on either side of the knot apart (Fig. A1-7). No other manipulation is necessary.

To dress a figure-of-eight on a bight, loosely tie the knot and then work out any twists or crosses (Fig. A1-8). Think of the rope strands as freeway lanes. Just like the lanes of a freeway, the cords should remain side by side, never crossing at any point along their path. When the crosses have been worked out, tighten the knot.

Figure A1-8. A loosely tied figure-of-eight on a bight.

Knots must also be firmly *tightened.* In most cases it's not enough to simply pull on the rope strands on either side of the knot in an effort to tighten it. With the figure-of-eight bend, for example, both strands on each side of the knot must be pulled tightly (four pulls total; Fig. A1-9).

Figure A1-9 Tightening a figure-of-eight bend.

Once a knot has been loaded, it can be difficult to loosen, especially if the rope is wet or icy. It's best to *break the strands* that run perpendicularly to the long axis of the knot away from the knot's center. Make sure to work both sides of the knot as shown in Figure A1-10.

Figure A1-10. Loosening a ring bend.

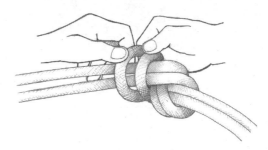

Bends, loops, and hitches are dressed and tightened differently, so know the specific ways to efficiently tie, dress, tighten, and loosen each knot. Keep in mind that working with tubular webbing is much different than tying knots with rope or accessory cord. Considerations for working with webbing are addressed below in the section Webbing Knots.

SUGGESTED KNOTS FOR TRAVEL AND RESCUE

Tie-in and Clip-in Knots

The most popular tie-in and clip-in knots are members of the figure-of-eight family. Figure-of-eight knots are the strongest used on a regular basis by climbers, they stay tied over the course of the day and are relatively easy to untie once loaded. When tying into the end of the rope use a *figure-of-eight follow-through* (Fig. A1-11). When clipping in to the end of the rope, use a *figure-of-eight on a bight* (Fig. A1-12). When tied, the result is the same, as shown below.

Figure A1-11. Tying a figure-of-eight follow-through.

Figure A1-12. Tying a figure-of-eight on a bight.

Some climbers question the decision to use a figure-of-eight on a bight as a means of attaching to the middle of the rope because the knot is split apart (hence weakened) during a crevasse fall. Others point out that the amount of stress on this knot during a crevasse fall is not that great, and that it's best to keep the number of knots required to a minimum.

A knot specifically designed to take a sideways force is the *butterfly knot*. It's the strongest middle person knot and it's easy to tie and untie (Fig. A1-13).

Begin by twisting two loops into the rope.

Pass the head of the outside loop over the rope and up through the center openings as shown above.

Dress the knot by pulling the rope strands on either side of the knot apart.

Figure A1-13. Tying a butterfly knot.

Some glacier travelers prefer to tie into the end of a rope with a double looped bowline (Fig. A1-14). It's easier to tie (and untie) than the figure-of-eight follow-through with gloves or mittens on. It's not, however, as secure as the figure-of-eight, so it's essential to finish the knot with a safety overhand.

Figure A1-14. Double looped bowline with a safety overhand knot.

Friction Knots

Friction knots are invaluable for glacier travel and rescue. They serve as ascending devices during a crevasse fall, as belay mechanisms during glacier travel, and as a means to transfer the load to an anchor during the rescue process.

There are many friction knots to choose from. Some are more appropriate than others in a given situation. In all cases, friction knots work the same way, by clamping on to the rope when tensioned, and sliding along the rope when tension is released (or allowing the rope to slide through the knot). In order for a friction knot to grip, the cord from which it is tied must be smaller in diameter than the rope to which it is attached (see see chapter 2). It also helps if the cord is relatively supple so that it can easily conform to the rope's circular shape.

The prusik knot is tied by wrapping consecutive girth hitches around the rope. A two-wrap prusik provides suffi-

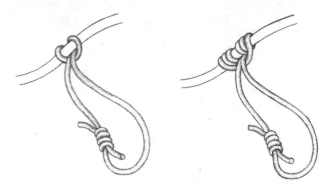

Figure A1-15. A three-wrap prusik. Tie three consecutive girth hitches. A single girth hitch is shown at left.

cient grip for ascending a rope. If the rope is icy, or if the load is heavier, a three-wrap prusik is necessary (Fig. A1-15). Always use a three-wrap prusik for rescue work.

Prusik knots tied with 1-inch tubular webbing slip on the rope, whereas prusiks tied with $^9/_{16}$-inch webbing hold fine, but are difficult to slide along the rope due to the small bulk. It is best to use accessory cord to tie a prusik knot.

The Klemheist knot works very well when tied with webbing (unlike the prusik knot). It's also faster to tie when using a long, 16- to 20-foot, cordelette, especially if the ends of the cordelette are left open (untied). Tying a prusik knot with a long cordelette is more time consuming, as the ends must be repeatedly passed through the knot.

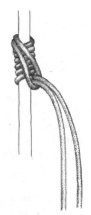

Figure A1-16. Klemheist knot.

The Bachmann Knot (Fig. A1-17) incorporates a carabiner as a handle, making it easier to slide the knot along the rope, a helpful feature when ascending a rope. The carabiner also enables the knot to be self-tending in a rescue system. This knot also works well when tied with webbing.

Useful Hitches

One of the most useful knots is the Müenter hitch. It is commonly used by the glacier traveler in lieu of a belay device and as a component of a tension

Figure A1-17. Bachmann knot.

release mechanism. It's advantageous to be able to tie this knot one handed, especially for a lone rescuer in self-arrest with only one hand free.

Use a locking carabiner when tying a Müenter hitch (Fig. A1-18). A pear-shaped carabiner may be needed to allow the knot to be flipped from one side of the carabiner to the other, especially when larger diameter rope is used.

Figure A1-18. Tying a one-handed Müenter hitch.

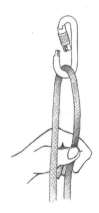 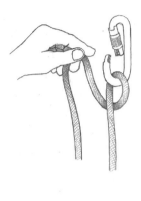 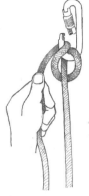

Grab the nonloaded strand and pass it behind the loaded strand.	Pull the strand up into a bight. Do not twist or flip this strand.	Clip the bight into the carabiner and lock the gate.

When used in a tension release mechanism, the Müenter hitch must be backed up. Tie a slippery hitch followed by a non-slippery overhand (Fig. A1-19) or a Müenter mule (Fig. A1-20).

Figure A1-19. Tying off a Müenter hitch.

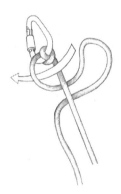  

Keep your brake hand on the rope! With your free hand, pull a bight around the loaded rope and through a slot formed immediately in front of the Müenter hitch.	The knot is now "slippery," meaning that the bight can easily be pulled out. For security, a slippery tie-off should always be backed up. An overhand on a bight is an excellent choice.	The finished product. Notice the overhand on a bight is snugged up against the slippery tie-off.

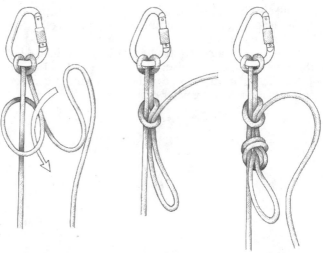

The Müenter mule is
started by tying an
overhand on a bight
around the loaded
strand.

The result is a "slippery"
knot that must be backed
up. The overhand on a
bight is an excellent
choice.

The finished
product.

The Mariner's hitch (Fig. A1-21) is a useful tension-release
knot. It's simple to tie, especially with an open-ended (untied)
cordelette. The major disadvantage to the Mariner's knot is
that it cannot be tied with a single strand of cord.

When tying the Mariner's hitch, wrap the cord twice
around the body of the carabiner and then around the strands
with a minimum of five wraps. Finish the knot off with a safety overhand.

Figure A1-21. Mariner's
hitch.

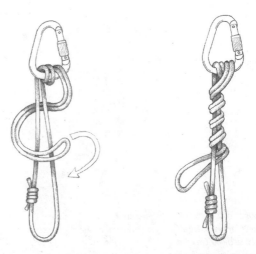

A clove hitch (Fig. A1-22) is an adjustable knot that grips
securely onto the round surface of a carabiner. The clove
hitch is particularly useful for attaching a sled to the rope or
when clipping into an anchor. In each case, the clove hitch is

a secure knot that allows for quick adjustment of the amount of slack or tension in the rope.

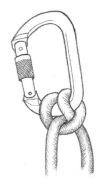

Figure A1-22. Tying a clove hitch.

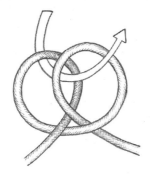

Using identical hand motions, tie two loops into the rope.

Slide one of the loops in front of the other. It will be clear which loop to slide as one choice results in a clove hitch and the other produces no knot at all. In this case, the loop on the right is slid in front of the loop on the left. Do not twist or fold the loop.

Clip the loops into a locking carabiner, tighten the hitch, and lock the gate.

Always use a locking carabiner when tying a clove hitch, and tighten the knot securely. A loose clove hitch can slip when loaded and weld abrade the rope. A loose knot can also detach from the carabiner. For these reasons some climbers favor the figure-of-eight on a bight as a method for attaching to an anchor. If you know how to tie a one-handed clove hitch, you can tie and adjust the knot at the same time (Fig. A1-23).

Figure A1-23. Tying a one-handed clove hitch.

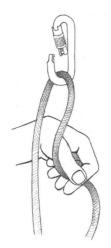

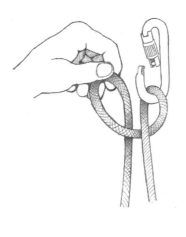

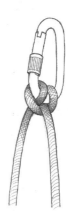

Pull the nonloaded strand behind the loaded one. Twist this strand into a loop.

You have two choices for twisting this strand. You'll always get it right if you twist the rope into a loop such that the length of the nonloaded strand ends up behind rather than in front of the loop.

Tighten the knot and lock the carabiner.

Other Useful Knots

One of the most secure knots is the grapevine (a.k.a. double fisherman's, Fig. A1-24). Climbers use it to join accessory cord, or even webbing, into slings. The knot definitely stays tied, especially once it is loaded.

Figure A1-24. Grapevine knot.

Begin by tying one end of the rope around the other end. Notice the X pattern formed.

Pass the working end between the X and the stationary strand of rope.

To adjust the length of end tail, slide the knot along the stationary strand. Tighten the knot.

Finish the other half of the grapevine by flipping the knot end to end and repeating the above sequence of hand motions.

Tying the knot is easier than it appears. Tie one side, flip the knot around and then tie the same knot again (using identical hand motions). The grapevine is tightened by pulling the strands on either side of the knot away from each other. It's tied properly when the four parallel strands are on the same side of the knot. If the parallel strands are opposite each other, a portion of the knot sticks out on either side, making these areas susceptible to abrasion.

The sheet bend (Fig. A1-25) is used to tie a Parisienne baudrier chest harness (see chapter 2).

Figure A1-25. Sheet bend.

The Garda knot (Fig. A1-26) is typically used for one-way hoisting. It locks the rope off at the end of each pull. The disadvantage of the Garda is that rope cannot be reversed through the carabiners. The Garda is best tied with two oval carabiners, because their symmetrical design prevents the carabiners from sliding off of each other.

 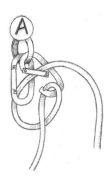 

Figure A1-26. Tying a Garda knot.

Clip the rope through both carabiners. In this case the loaded strand is on the right.

Clip the rope back through the first carabiner. When tied correctly the nonloaded (belay) strand runs between the carabiners.

When the loaded (right) strand is weighted, the rope is pinched between the two carabiners, preventing movement. When the loaded strand is unweighted, slack can be pulled through the system.

Webbing Knots

Overhand knots are used almost exclusively when working with sling webbing. The water knot (ring bend; Fig. A1-27) is used to join pieces of webbing into slings or runners.

Figure A1-27. Water knot (ring bend).

The water knot has an uncanny ability to work itself loose over time. Dressing the knot properly, as shown in Figure A1-28, adds to its security. Get in the habit of checking the water knot frequently. It's also a good idea to incorporate long (at least 3 inch) tails into the knot when tying it.

Figure A1-28. Dressing a water knot.

To dress the water knot, pinch the webbing on each side of the knot and then give each strand a good tug. The finished product will look like a tie.

It's also possible to use a grapevine knot to join webbing into runners. The grapevine cinches tightly when loaded, adding an element of security lacking with the water knot. The grapevine, however, may be impossible to untie once loaded, a definite disadvantage when trying to tie runners together. Some climbers carry a selection of runners joined with water knots and grapevines in order to take advantage of the benefits of each knot.

Tie an overhand on-a-bight (Fig. A1-29) to form a loop in the middle of a runner, or in one end of an individual strand of webbing (for girth-hitching a piece of webbing to a prusik in a tension-release mechanism).

Figure A1-29. Overhand on-a-bight at the end of a sling.

The Self-Arrest APPENDIX 2

The purpose of the self-arrest is to stop a personal slip that cannot be contained by a self-belay, or to hold the fall of a ropemate who is out of control. In the context of glacier travel, the self-arrest is the primary means of stopping a ropemate's forceful crevasse fall. Since falls can happen in an instant, you must develop a skilled, instinctive self-arrest response. The life of your teammates may very well be in your hands in this moment of crisis!

The key to developing an effective self-arrest response is practice. Like CPR, it's a skill that can get rusty when not used, so make a habit of practicing at the beginning of every mountaineering season until your arrest is razor-sharp. The following suggestions will get you started:

- Select a practice slope with a long, safe run-out, one that allows you to come to a complete stop after a toboggan-type ride. Avoid slopes above rock piles or other physical hazards. Check the slope out before using it. Look for rocks or any other hazards that are hidden by a thin surface layer of snow.

- Start on a slope steep enough to slide on, but not so steep that your slide will be a rocket ride to the bottom. A slope with well-consolidated snow is best. When the snow is soft, you may have to create a chute in order to get sufficient speed up. Avoid ice slopes. They make poor practice venues, not to mention the fact that a self-arrest is not designed to stop a fall on ice. As your skill improves, you can transition to progressively steeper slopes.

- Dress for comfort and safety. You're going to get wet, so wear a rain jacket, waterproof pants, and gaiters. Mitten shells will help keep your hand layer dry. Top it off with a well-fitted and adjusted helmet. Do not wear a poncho or any other garment that may interfere with your self-arrest.

- Keep your axe tether off while practicing. If you make a mistake, your axe will not be attached to you. Do not wear crampons!

- Hold your axe with a self-arrest grip because it allows you to initiate the arrest without changing your hand position. Chapter 2 describes the merits and limitations of holding the axe with either the self-arrest or self-belay grip.

- Learn how to arrest from all possible body orientations and while carrying a large pack. Your self-arrest reaction must be correct and instinctive, regardless of body orientation.

- Be aggressive. A tenacious attitude comes in handy during a fall that is difficult to stop. Continue arresting any fall until it's contained.

The Basic Self-Arrest Position

Figure A2-1. The self-arrest grip.

Your axe should always be held in the proper position for self-arrest. When you fall, the initial axe position will be different for each body orientation, but the end position is the same: axe across the chest with the spike out to the side of the hip, as shown in Figure A2-1.

Feet-First Fall

The self-arrest should initially be practiced by falling feet first while facing down the slope (Fig. A2-2).

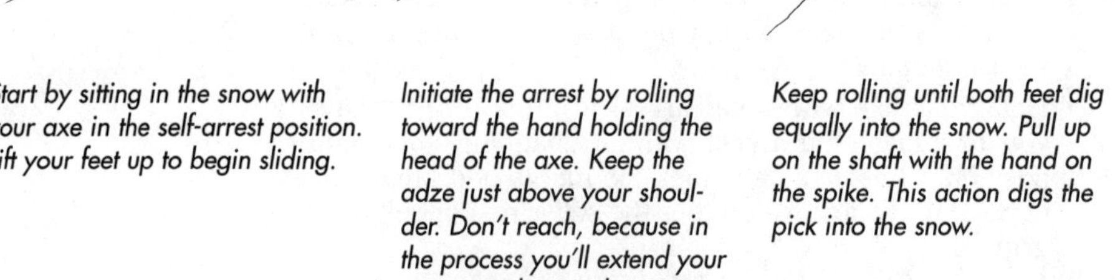

Start by sitting in the snow with your axe in the self-arrest position. Lift your feet up to begin sliding.

Initiate the arrest by rolling toward the hand holding the head of the axe. Keep the adze just above your shoulder. Don't reach, because in the process you'll extend your arms, weakening the arrest and increasing the chances of losing control of the axe.

Keep rolling until both feet dig equally into the snow. Pull up on the shaft with the hand on the spike. This action digs the pick into the snow.

Figure A2-2. The feet-first fall.

Head-First Downhill on the Stomach

Start by lying on your stomach facing downhill. Someone may have to hold your feet while you get into position. Begin sliding.

Plant the axe pick to initiate the self-arrest. This creates a pivot point around which your body will rotate. Keep the shaft of the axe below chin level and your head up!

 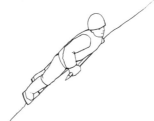

Keep your feet up as your body pivots around the axe placement. Pull up with the lower hand to keep the spike from digging into the snow.

When your body swings completely around, dig your feet in and pull up on the spike of the axe until you come to a complete stop.

Figure A2-3. Falling head-first downhill on the stomach.

Head-First Downhill on the Back

Figure A2-4. Falling head-first downhill on the back.

Start by lying on your back facing downhill. Begin sliding. Plant the axe pick by your hip to initiate the self-arrest, creating a pivot point.

Keep your feet up as your body pivots around the axe placement.

Bending at the hips into a pike position helps you bring your legs around into a downhill orientation.

Finish of the self-arrest in the normal fashion.

Self-Arrest with a Large Pack

Self-arresting with a large pack is cumbersome. Not only will it be more awkward, but also the momentum generated can make the arrest difficult to contain. Special consideration must be given to a head-first fall on the back with a large pack on. You won't be able to arrest the fall in the usual fashion—by digging the pick into the snow by your hip because you're too far from the snow surface. Roll over onto your stomach first and begin the arrest from this position, as shown in Figure A2-5.

Starting the arrest by digging the pick into the snow by your hip won't work; you're too far above the snow surface!

Roll over into a head-first downhill position.

Twist the pick around until it's in position to bite into the snow and pull up with the lower hand to keep the spike from digging in.

Keep your feet up as you rotate around the axe pick. Keep the axe head close to your shoulder.

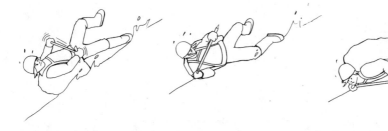

Starting the arrest by digging the pick into the snow by your hip will not work; you are too far above the snow surface.

Roll over into a head-first stomach position.

Twist the pick around until it's in position to bite into the snow. Pull up with the lower hand to keep the spike from digging in.

Keep your feet up as you rotate around the pick. Keep your axe head close to your shoulder.

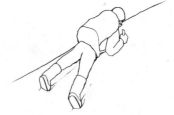

When you are aligned vertically on the slpe, dig your feet in and finish the arrest off in the usual manner.

Figure A2-5. Self-arrest with a heavy pack.

Common Self-Arrest Mistakes

There are a number of mistakes that climbers make while self-arresting. Have a climbing partner observe your self-arrest technique, looking for any of the common errors identified in Table A2-1.

Table A2-1. Solutions to Common Self-Arrest Errors

Problem	Possible Cause	Solution	Concerns
Losing control of the head of the axe.	Reaching for the self-arrest.	Roll into the self-arrest and brace the arm holding the head of the axe. The adze must remain just above shoulder level.	It's remarkably easy to dislocate your shoulder when the pick bites into snow that has very little give. Practice on solid snow from a foot-first fall. Start with short slides and increase the slide length when skill improves.
	The pick grabs and jerks the axe forcefully.	Roll the pick into self-arrest position so that it doesn't bite and jerk the axe away from you.	
Rolling the incorrect way into arrest.	Lack of concentration or disorientation.	More practice.	When you roll into the spike (rather than the head of the axe) you have a greater distance to roll and in the process you'll gain more speed. You may also plant the spike and get launched into the air.
Arresting while on the side rather than with the torso facing the snow.	A combination of things: digging in with just one foot, impatience, poor technique that was not initially corrected.	Complete the roll onto the shaft of the axe, dig in with both feet, get your rear end up in the air, and pull up with the hand on the spike end.	When you arrest from the side it's difficult to get your torso fully over the axe, making it more difficult to stop a demanding fall.
The spike bites into the snow when you're sliding in a head-first fall.	Poor control of the shaft of the axe by the hand on the spike end of the axe.	Pull up with the hand on the spike to keep it from biting into the snow.	If the spike bites into the snow you could lose the grip on the axe or sustain an injury, especially when the axe is in front of your face in a head-first on the stomach fall.

Suggestions for Making Self-Arrest Practice More Challenging

Once you've learned the basics, increase the rigor of practice sessions. A word of caution before you start. Make sure your self-arrest is solid and you're comfortable executing it in all body orientations before trying any of the following drills.

- Etch a line into the slope delineating a makeshift "crevasse of doom." Start sliding and do not self-arrest until a partner yells "arrest!" Try to stop yourself from going over the cliff.
- Give your axe to a partner who gets into position down the slope and just off to the side of your slide path. Grab the axe on your way past and self-arrest as fast as you can. While this is a suitable drill for feet-first and head-first on the back slides, do not attempt it while sliding head-first on the stomach. You could easily knock out some teeth. For an added challenge, add in the crevasse of doom.
- While holding your axe in self-arrest position run down the slope until you lose control. Arrest the fall as fast as you can.
- Rope in with a partner. Sit together, one above the other, at the top of the slope with the rope stacked between you. Send your partner down the slope without arresting. When the rope comes taut you'll be jerked down the slope. Arrest the fall. Begin on a short rope and progressively increase the distance between attachment points. Or add another ropemate and send both of them down the slope without arresting. Arrest their falls. After some practice, you'll develop a very good idea of how hard it can be to stop a rope team. Of course, slope gradient and surface conditions will affect your ability to stop such a fall.

Self-Arrests and Crampons

For obvious reasons you should never practice the self-arrest with your feet down while wearing crampons. You should never get your feet anywhere near the snow surface when wearing them, for if you catch a point you could easily snap an ankle. If you fall while wearing crampons, you must have the presence of mind to keep your feet up. This requires a conditioned response; you won't have much time to think about what to do.

For this reason, some climbers advocate learning how to arrest from the knees. It's uncomfortable and the self-arrest is not as effective, but a habitual response of keeping your toes (and thus your ankles) out of harm's way is developed from the outset. Other climbers believe that the self-arrest should be learned with the feet down because the self-arrest is a technique used for stopping a fall on snow only.

If you've learned to self-arrest with the feet down and have not developed a response to a fall with crampons, we highly recommend that you spend some time self-arresting from the knees. Sooner or later you're bound to fall when wearing crampons.

Mechanical Advantage

Rescuers would be hard pressed to pull a team member from a crevasse without the application of mechanical advantage. A rescue system incorporating mechanical advantage multiplies the pulling force and makes it possible to raise a heavy load with less effort than might otherwise be required. This is a boon to the rescue team short on pulling power. Mechanical advantage is best expressed as a set of ratios:

$$\frac{\text{Pounds of Lift}}{\text{Pound of Pull}}$$ This ratio expresses how many pounds of lift are derived per pound of pull. With a 3:1 system, a climber weighing 180 pounds can be raised with 60 pounds of pull, at least in theory. In actuality, friction in the system reduces the efficiency of a 3:1 system to about 2:1 without rescue pulleys. Even when pulleys are used, mechanical advantage is much less than its theoretical value.

$$\frac{\text{Amount of Rope Pulled}}{\text{Distance of Lift Achieved}}$$ The distance the climber is raised is proportional to the amount of rope pulled through any rescue system incorporating mechanical advantage. For example, in a 3:1 system, three feet of rope is pulled through the system for every one foot of lift achieved.

The best rescue system is not necessarily the one that uses the greatest mechanical advantage. There comes a point when the benefits gained from additional mechanical advantage are outweighed by the increase in the amount of rope that must be pulled through the system. For this reason, rescuers seldom use anything more than a 6:1 system. It's usually best to use the simplest system possible, to reduce the set-up time and minimize the amount of required equipment. From a safety perspective, a simpler system is easier to assess and monitor.

COMMON RESCUE SYSTEMS

The 1:1 System

As the name implies, the 1:1 system provides no mechanical advantage. Every pound of pull exerted lifts a pound of the climber's weight, and for every foot of lift, a foot of rope is pulled through the system. When any load is fully supported by a rope, it is a 1:1.

Figure A3-1. The 1:1 system.

As Figure A3-1 shows, in a 1:1 system the rope simply changes direction around a pulley or carabiner. It's important to be able to quickly recognize changes of direction when estimating the amount of force applied to different components of the system (e.g., the anchor). In both of these examples, the anchor must support the weight of the climber and the counterbalancing force applied by the rescuer.

C-Pulley

The c-pulley is a 2:1 system (Fig. A3-2). It's easily recognized because one end of the rope is always anchored. In a 2:1 system, the anchored strand supports half of the load, while the rescuers support the other half.

C-Pulley on a C-Pulley

A c-pulley can be added to another c-pulley, providing a 4:1 system.

In this example, a second c-pulley is attached to the initial c-pulley. Notice that the end of each c-pulley set-up is anchored. Let's examine this system a little more closely. Assume a 200 pound load is being lifted. The pull strand of the initial c-pulley supports half of the load, or 100 pounds. This means that 100 pounds are transferred to the second c-pulley system, with the anchored

Figure A3-2. The c-pulley.

Figure A3-3. C-pulley on a c-pulley.

and pull strands each accepting half of the load (50 pounds). Thus, 50 pounds of pull are required to lift 200 pounds.

It is important to know how much force is transferred to the anchor when hauling with any rescue system. In the above 4:1 system only 50 pounds are required to lift a 200-pound climber. Does this means that the difference (150 pounds) is transferred to the anchor? Let's answer this by looking at this system from another perspective, by calculating how much force is placed on the anchor via each of the anchored strands. The anchor strand of the initial c-pulley supports half of the climber's weight, or 100 pounds. The anchor strand of the second c-pulley also supports half of its load, or 50 pounds. So, the answer is yes, with 50 pounds of pull, the anchor supports the remaining 150 pounds! Keep in mind, however, that these are theoretical values. Friction intensifies the load on all points.

Z-Pulley

The z-pulley is the most commonly used rescue system, combining a 1:1 and a 2:1 system (Fig. A3-4). It provides 3:1 theoretical mechanical advantage.

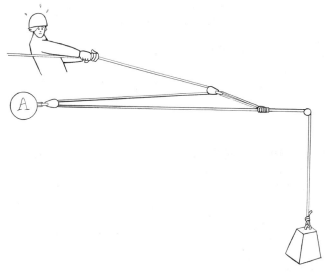

Figure A3-4. The z-pulley.

Figure A3-5 illustrates the theoretical forces at work in the system. Notice that 70 pounds of force are required to raise the 210-pound load. As the figure shows, the z-pulley consists of two significant changes of direction. At each of these changes of direction, forces are transferred: first to the sliding pulley and its attachment to the haul prusik ($F1 + F2 = F4 = 140$ pounds); second, to the fixed pulley and its attachment to the anchor ($F2 + F3 = F5 = 140$ pounds). Adding the forces

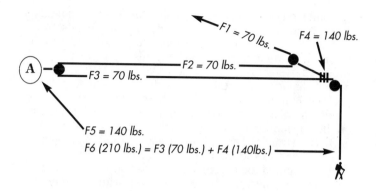

Figure A3-5. The forces at work in a z-pulley.

applied along the entire length of the rope reveals the following: The initial 70 pounds of pull are transferred around both of the changes of direction and along the rope to the point where the haul prusik is attached to the rope. At this point, the 70 pounds of pull couple with the 140 pounds of force transferred to the sliding pulley and haul prusik, resulting in 210 pounds of theoretical force applied to the load.

In order to maximize mechanical advantage, use pulleys and pull in as straight a line as possible. In the absence of pulleys, use two carabiners at each 180-degree bend in the rope. Friction is much greater with only one carabiner. If only one pulley is available, connect it to the haul prusik. This is where pulling efforts are concentrated. More rope also passes through the sliding pulley than around a pulley attached to the anchor.

Z-Pulley with a Ratchet Prusik

When the climber is raised with a z-pulley, the sliding pulley and haul prusik are pulled closer to the anchor until a point is reached where pulling any farther results in a potential loss in leverage. The addition of a ratchet prusik to the anchor allows the climber to be supported while the sliding pulley is reset farther down the rope (Fig. A3-6).

The 6:1 System

A c-pulley can be added to a z-pulley to create a 6:1 pulley system. In this case, the two systems are joined by tying a loop in the pull strand of the z-pulley, attaching a carabiner and pulley to this loop and clipping the c-pulley to this set-up (Fig. A3-6).

The 2:1 system (in effect) doubles the amount of mechanical advantage applied by the z-pulley. The main disadvantage of the 6:1 system is that 6 feet of rope must be pulled through the system for a single foot of lift. A lone rescuer will, however, be less concerned with the amount of rope that must be pulled and more appreciative of the relative ease with which a climber can be raised from a crevasse.

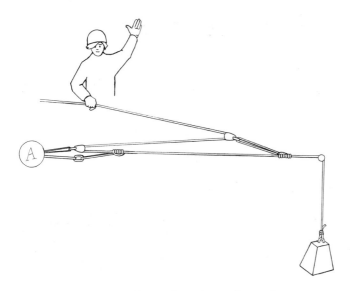

Figure A3-6. The z-pulley with a ratchet prusik.

It's also possible to add a z-pulley to a c-pulley (rather than a c-pulley to a z-pulley). The system illustrated in chapter 6 combines the two systems in this manner.

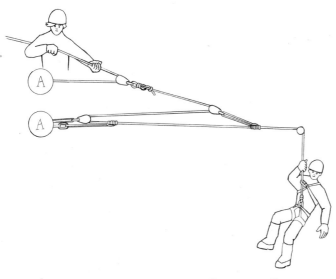

Figure A3-7. The 6:1 system—c-pulley on a z-pulley.

Bibliography

Barry, John and Mear, Roger. *Climbing School.* New York: Barron's, 1989.

Fyffe, Allen and Peter, Iain. *The Handbook of Climbing.* London, England: Pelham Books/Stephen Greene Press, 1990.

Graydon, D. and Hanson, K., eds. *Mountaineering: The Freedom of the Hills,* 6th ed. Seattle: The Mountaineers, 1997.

March, Bill. *Modern Rope Techniques in Mountaineering.* Milnthorpe, England: Cicerone Press, 1990.

Powers, Phil. *NOLS Wilderness Mountaineering.* Mechanicsburg, Pa.: Stackpole Books, 1993.

Selters, Andy. *Glacier Travel and Crevasse Rescue,* 2nd ed. Seattle: The Mountaineers, 1999.

Sharp, Robert P. *Glaciers.* Eugene: University of Oregon Press, 1960.

About the Authors and Illustrator

Michael Strong, former National Outdoor Leadership School instructor, has been alpine climbing for more than twenty years. He currently directs the Outdoor Pursuits Program at the University of Oregon and teaches ice, rock, and alpine climbing as well as courses in mountain rescue, avalanche safety, high angle rescue, and glacier rigging and rescue.

Eck Doerry has climbed alpine routes in Alaska, the Cascades, the Sierras, and the rockies and has taught alpine climbing and mountain rescue techniques for numerous outdoor schools.

Ryan Ojerio is a professional illustrator and climber.